This Book Belongs To:

____

Celtic Alphabet Coloring Book

Posh Pages

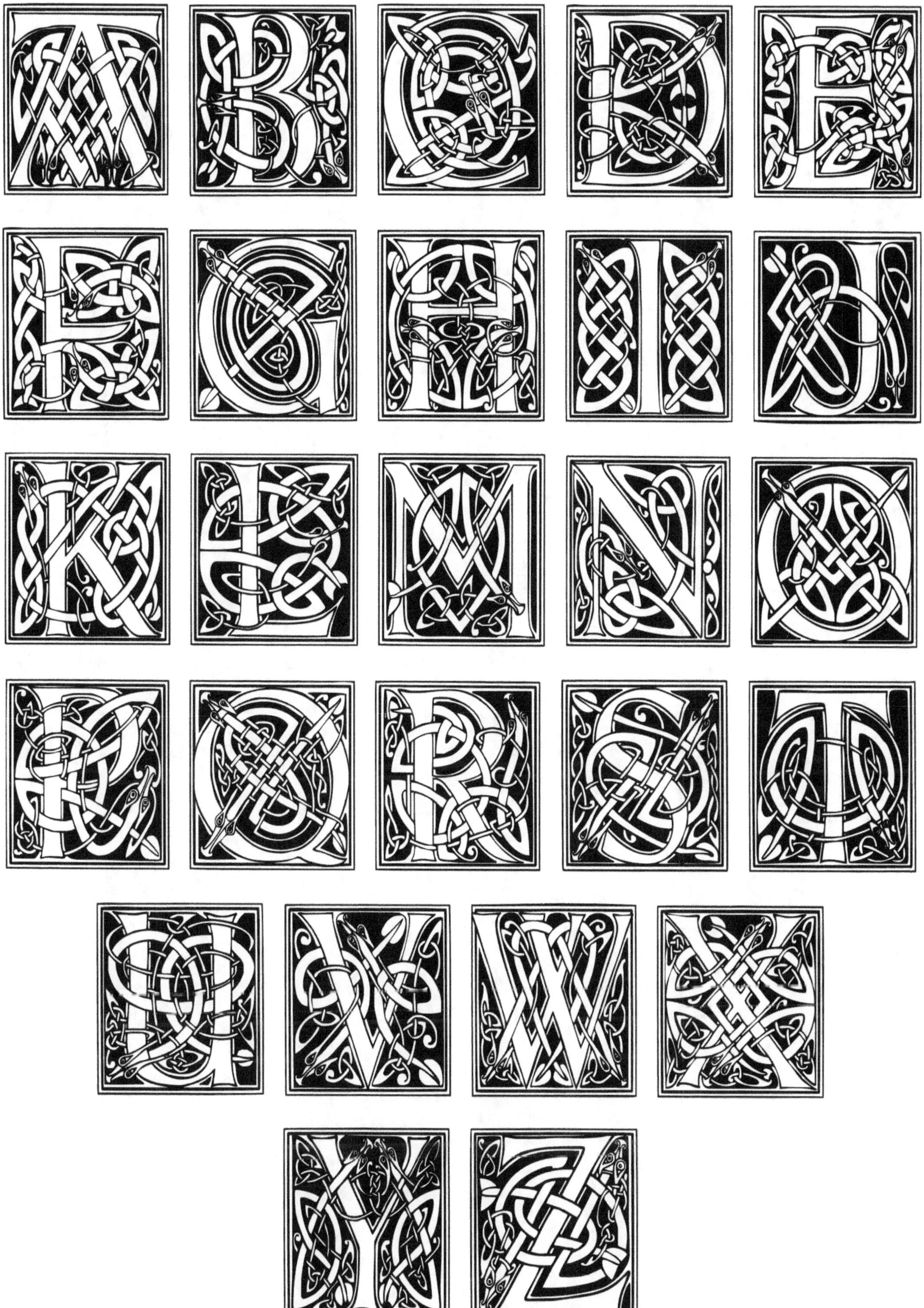

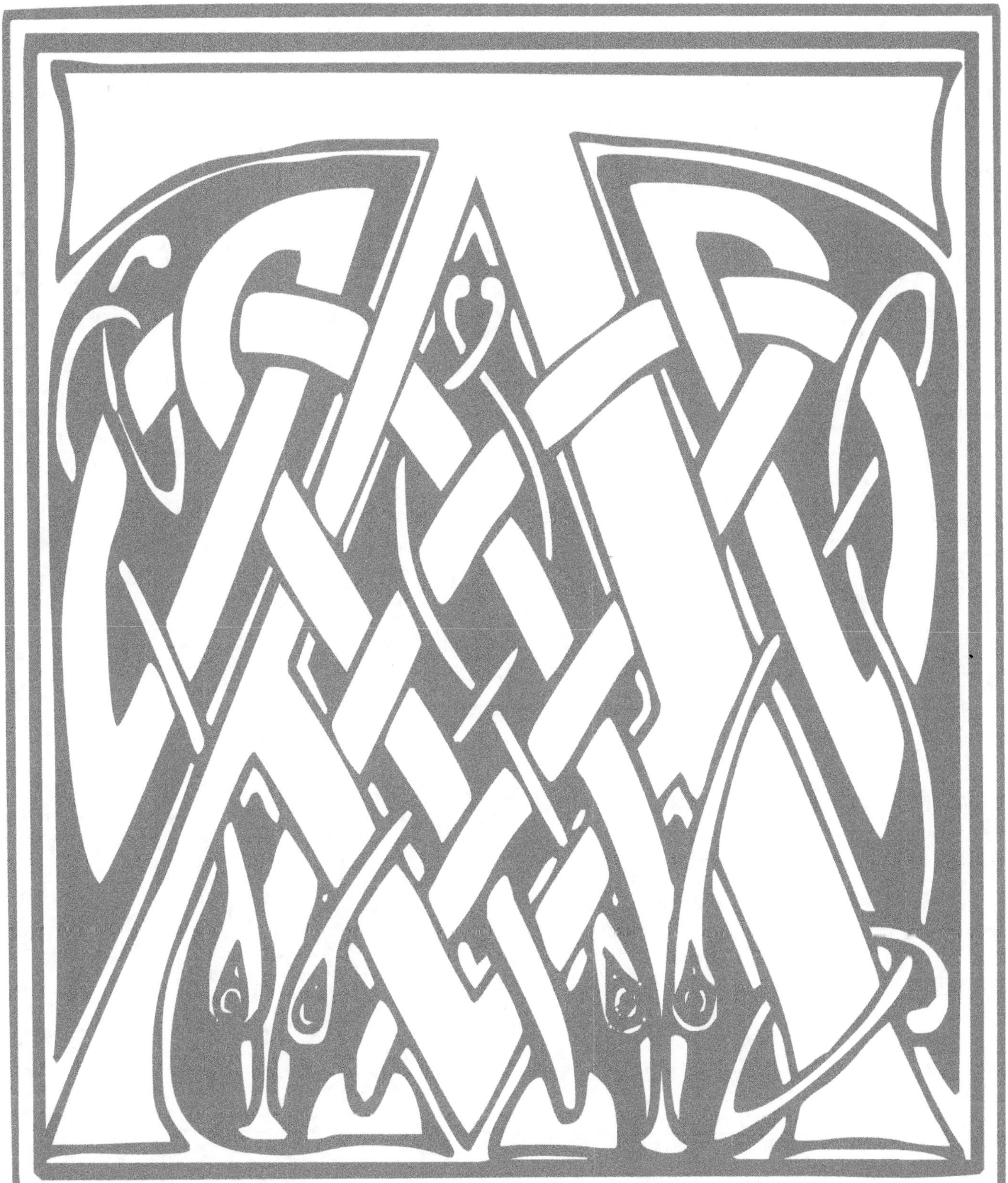

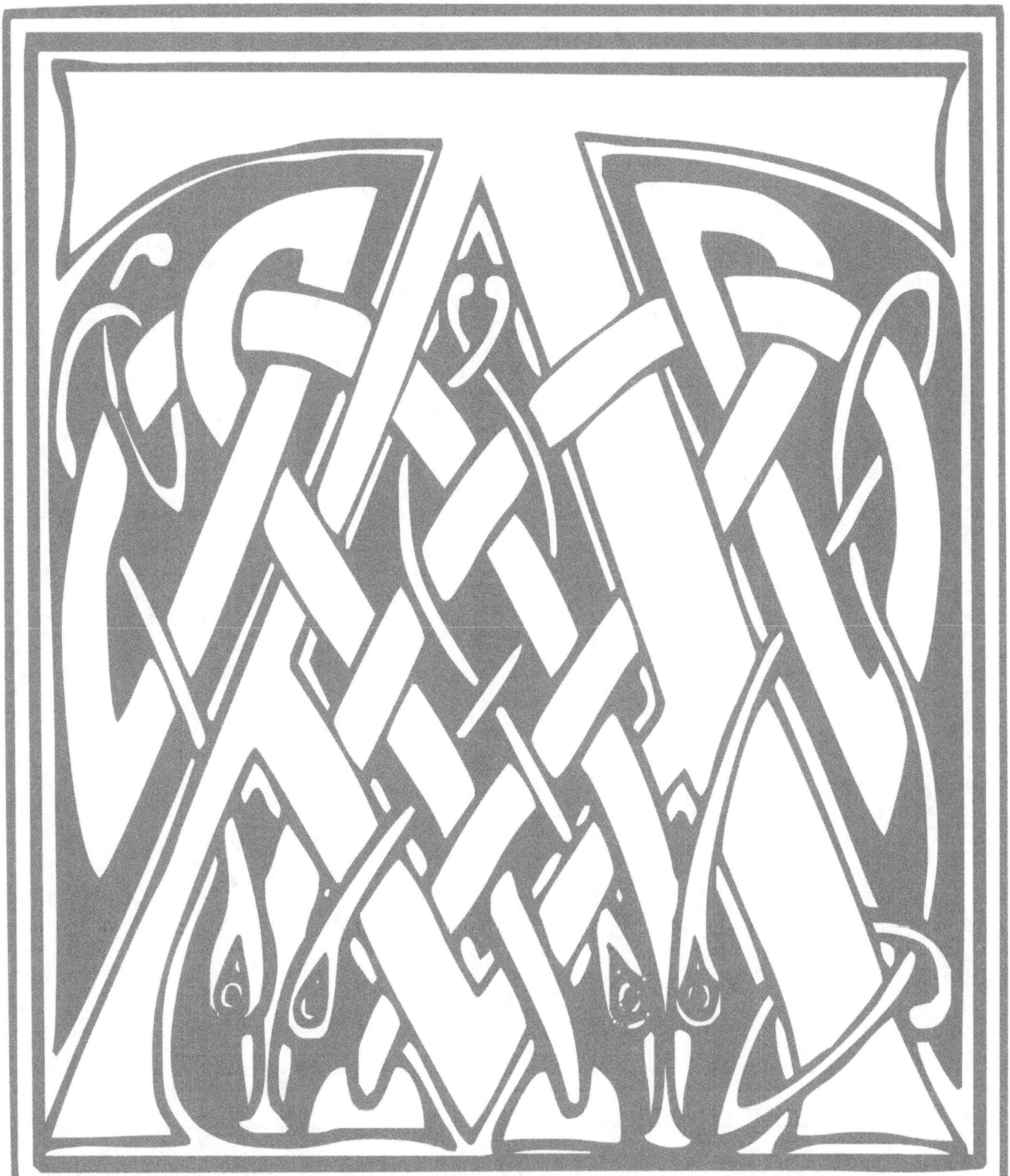

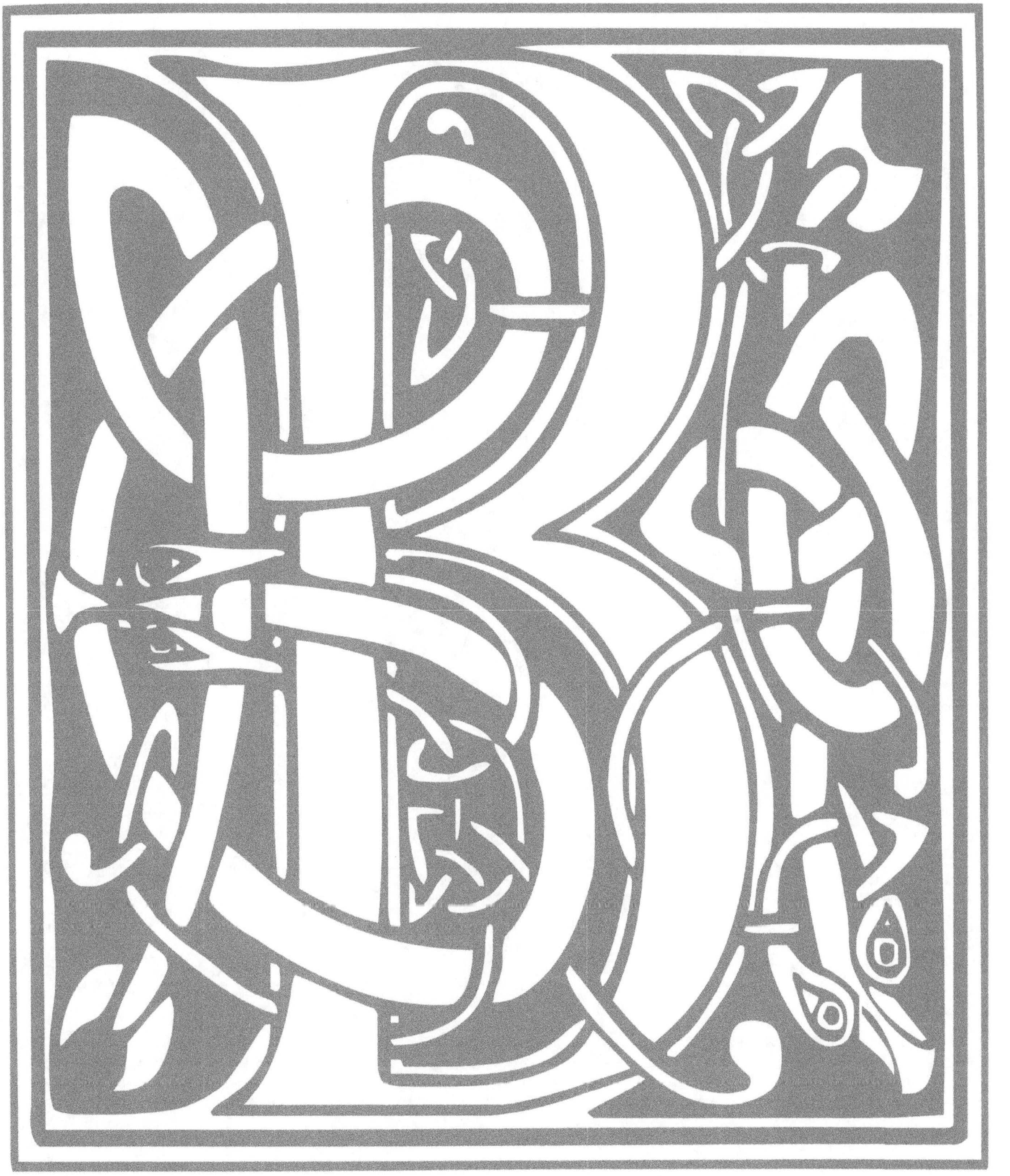

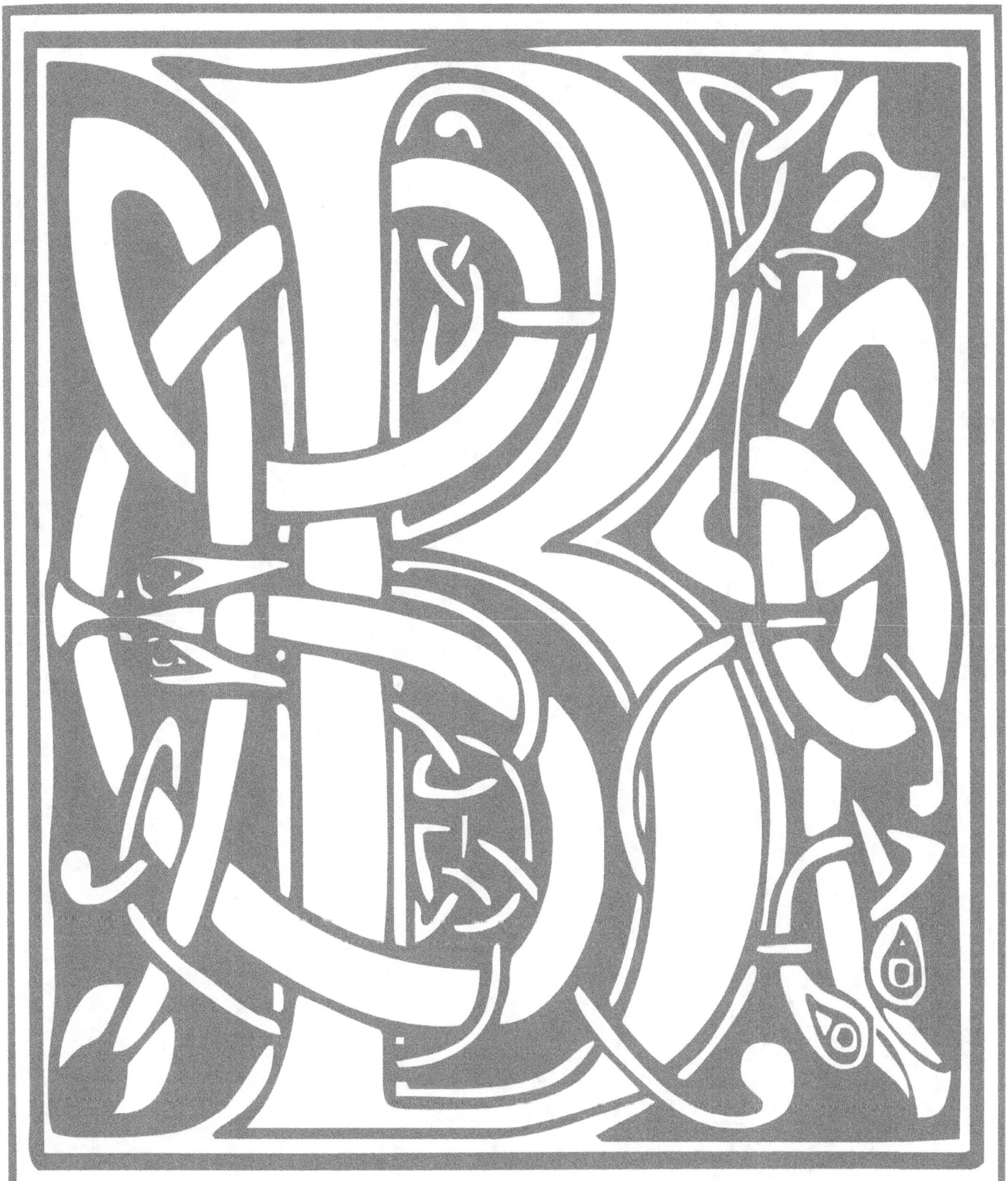

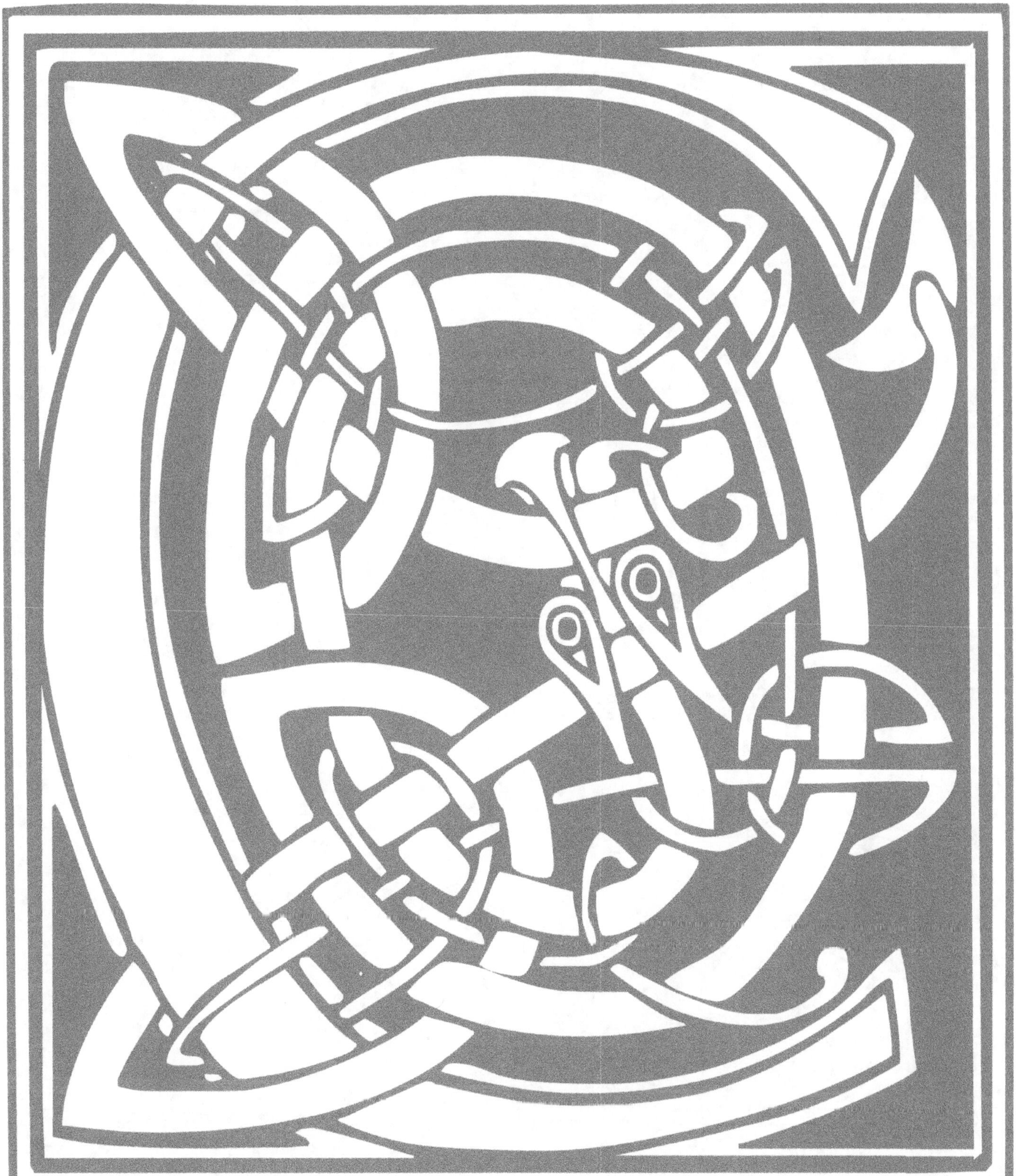

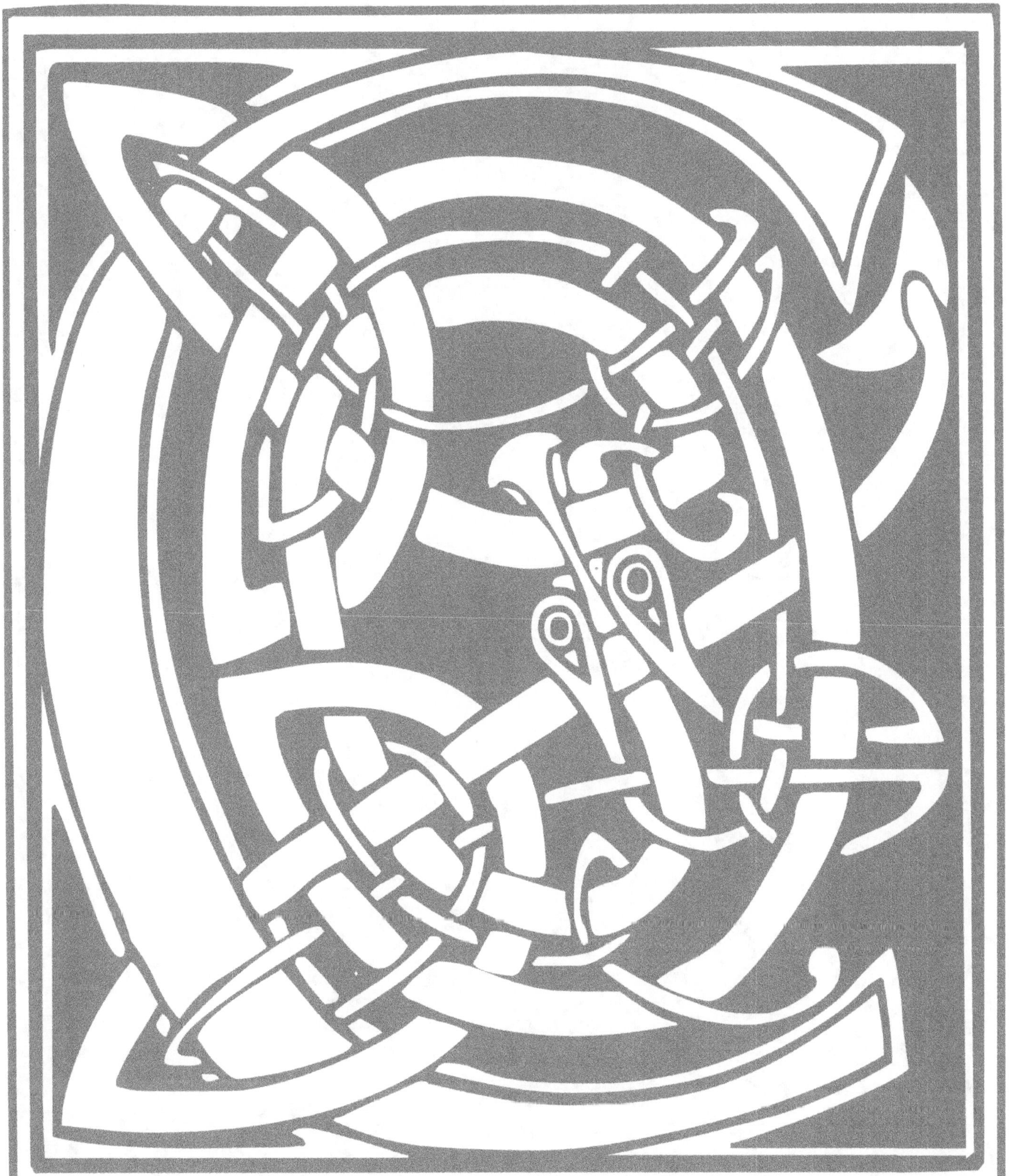

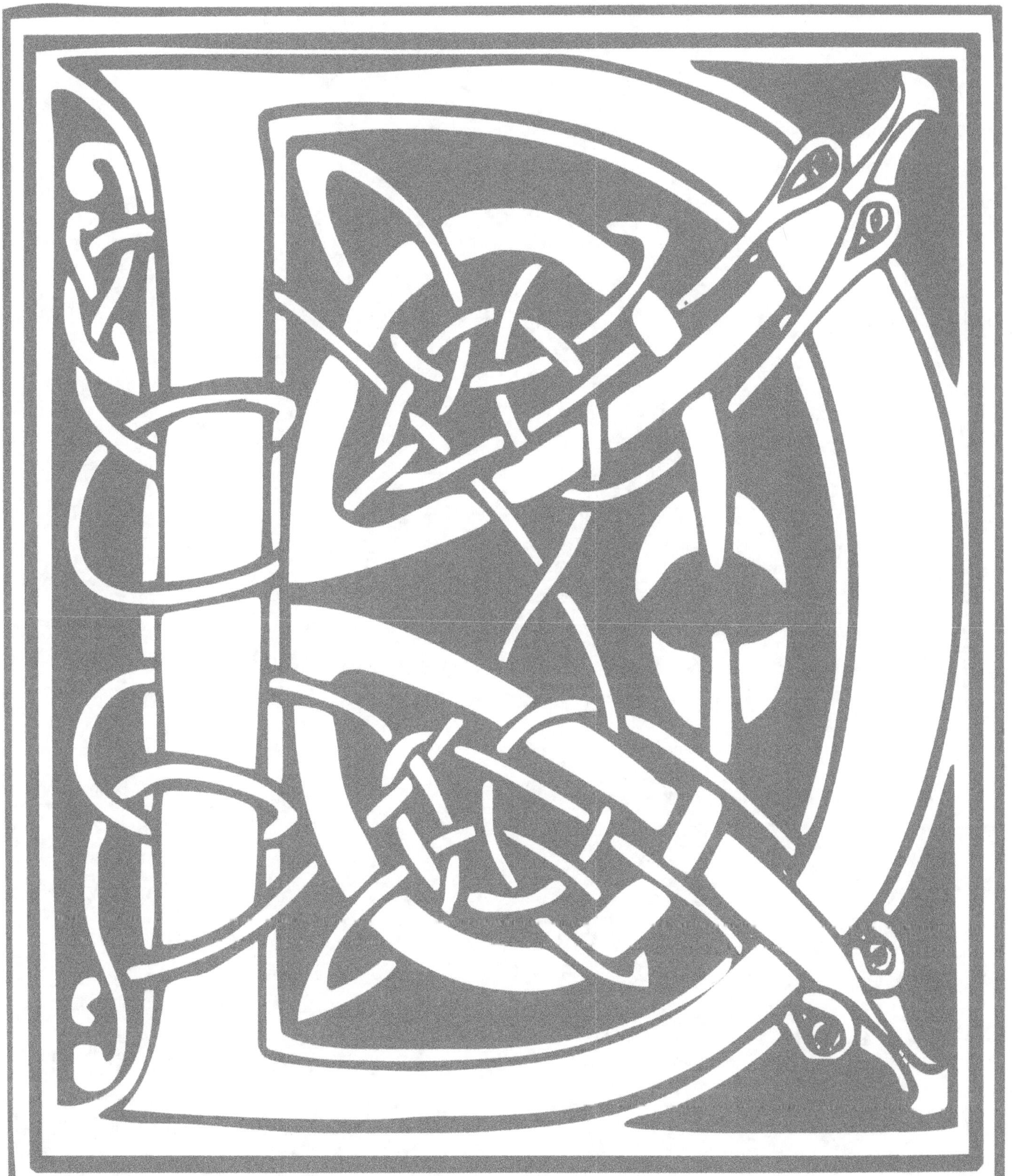

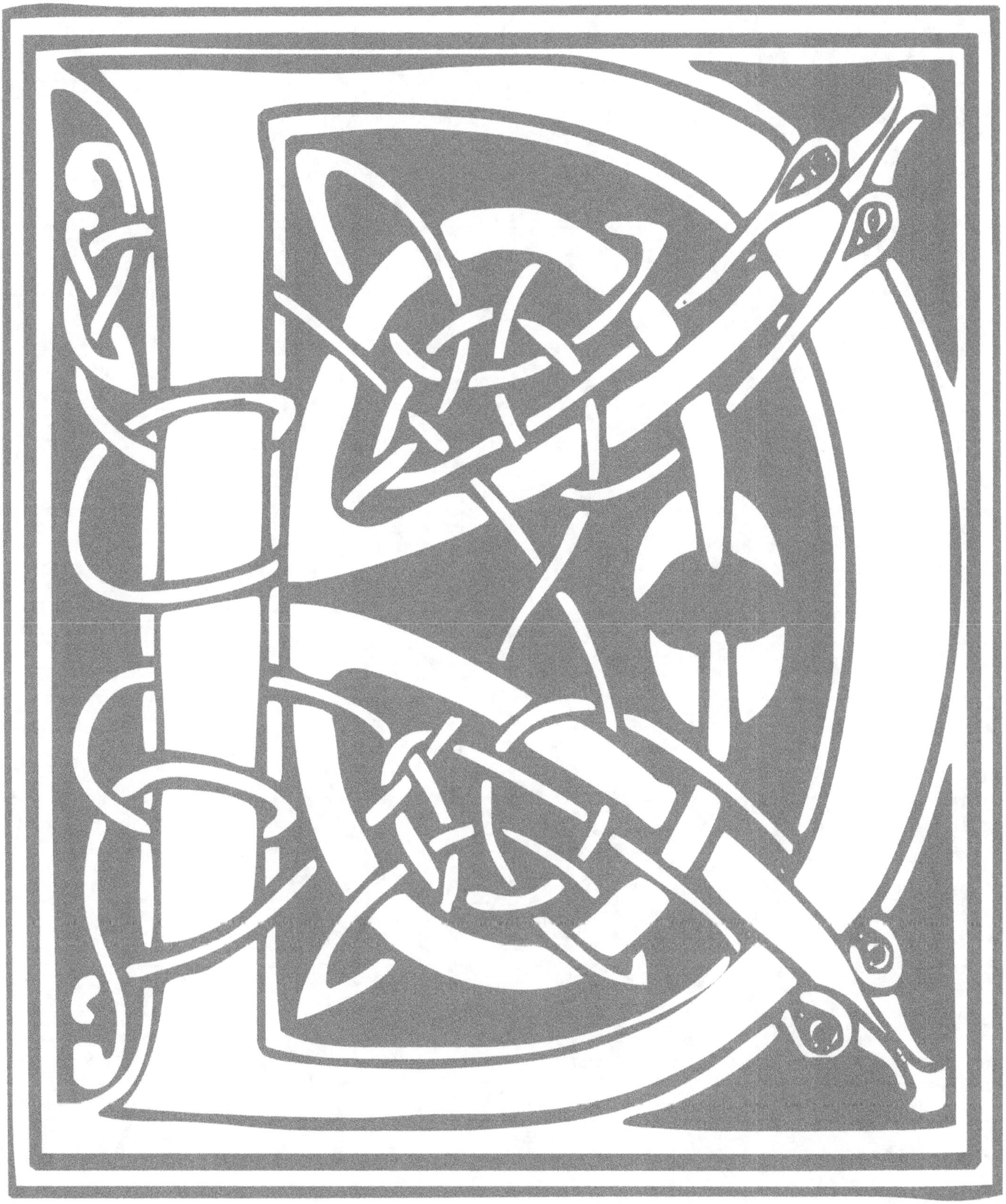

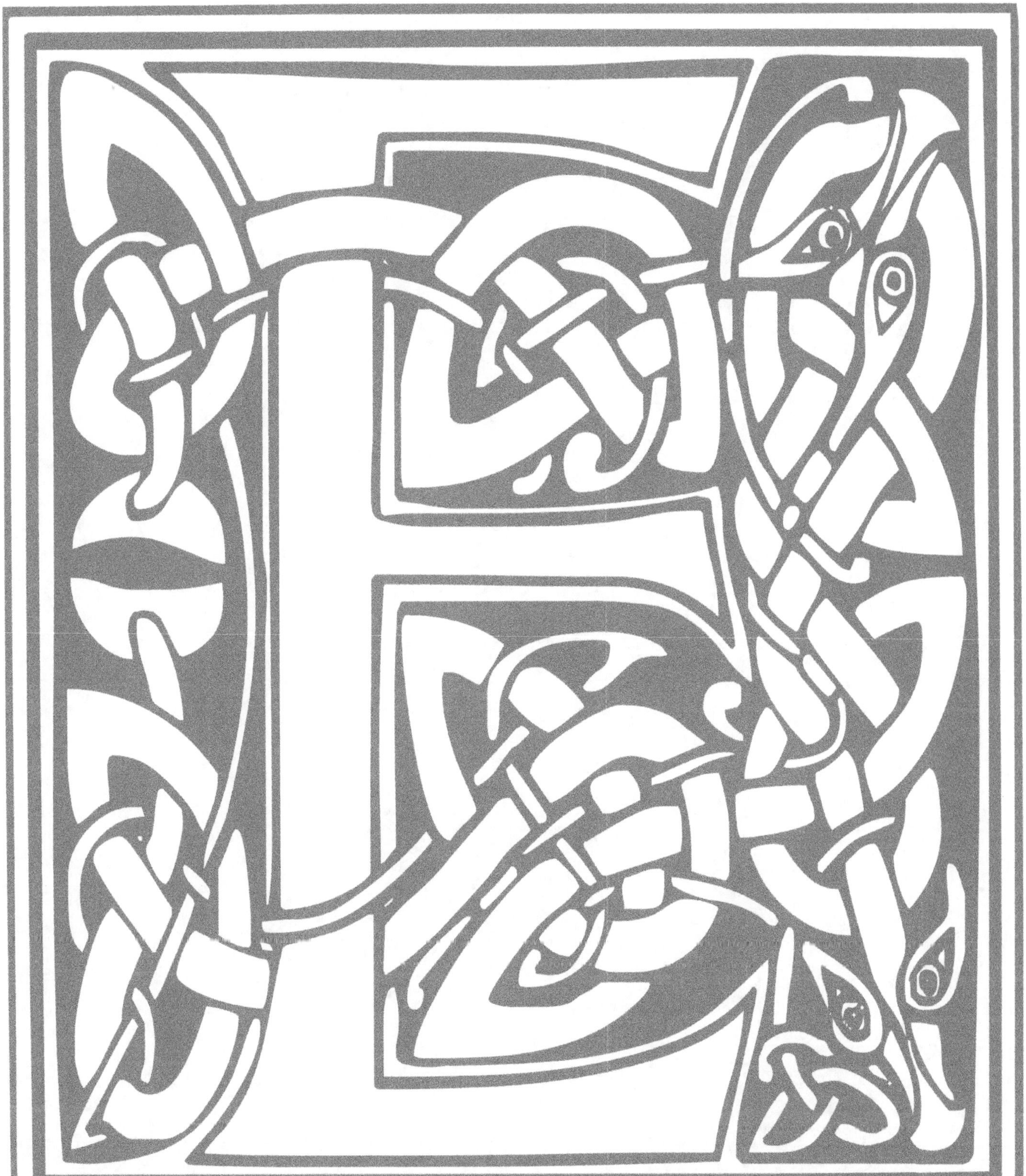

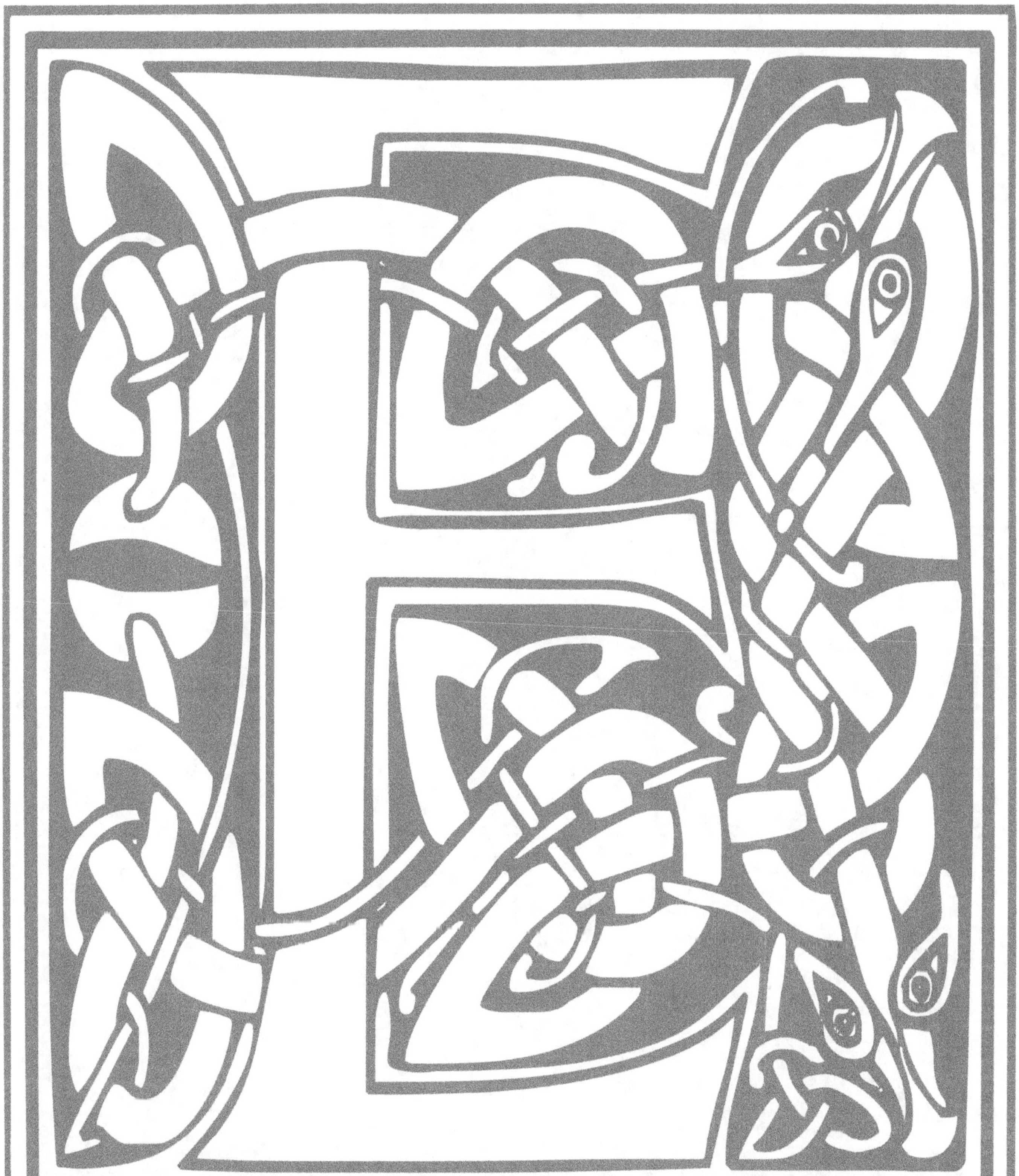

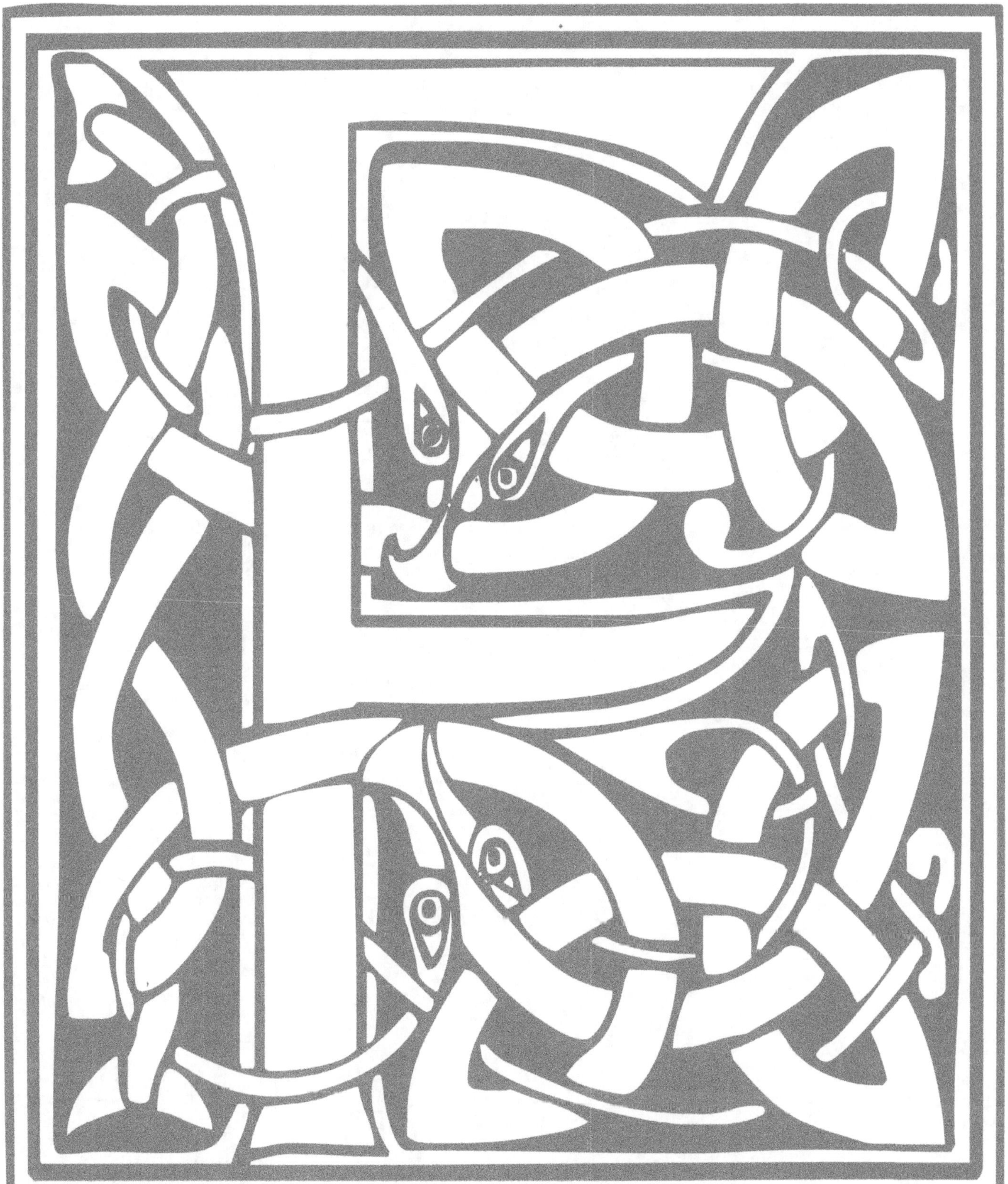

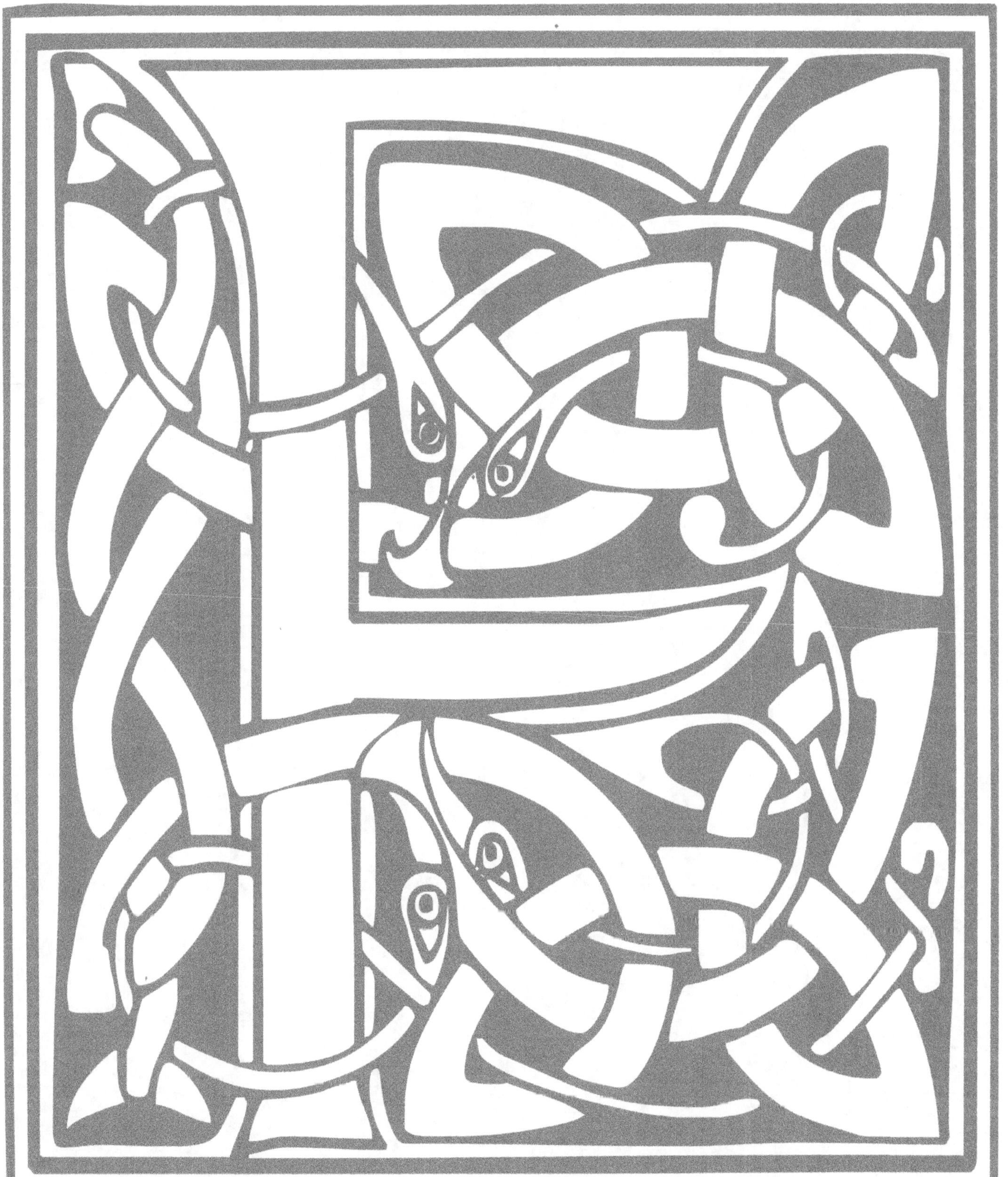

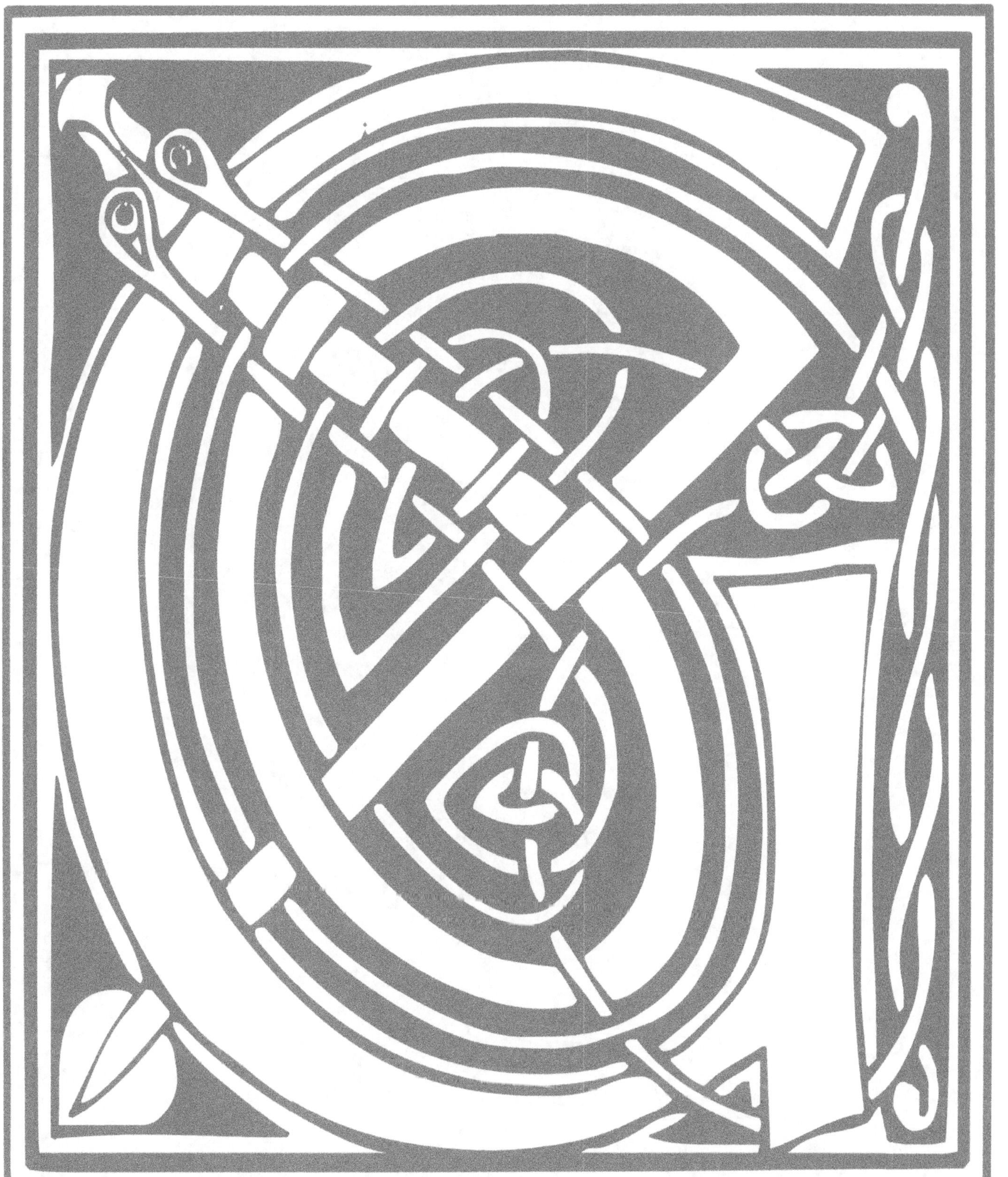

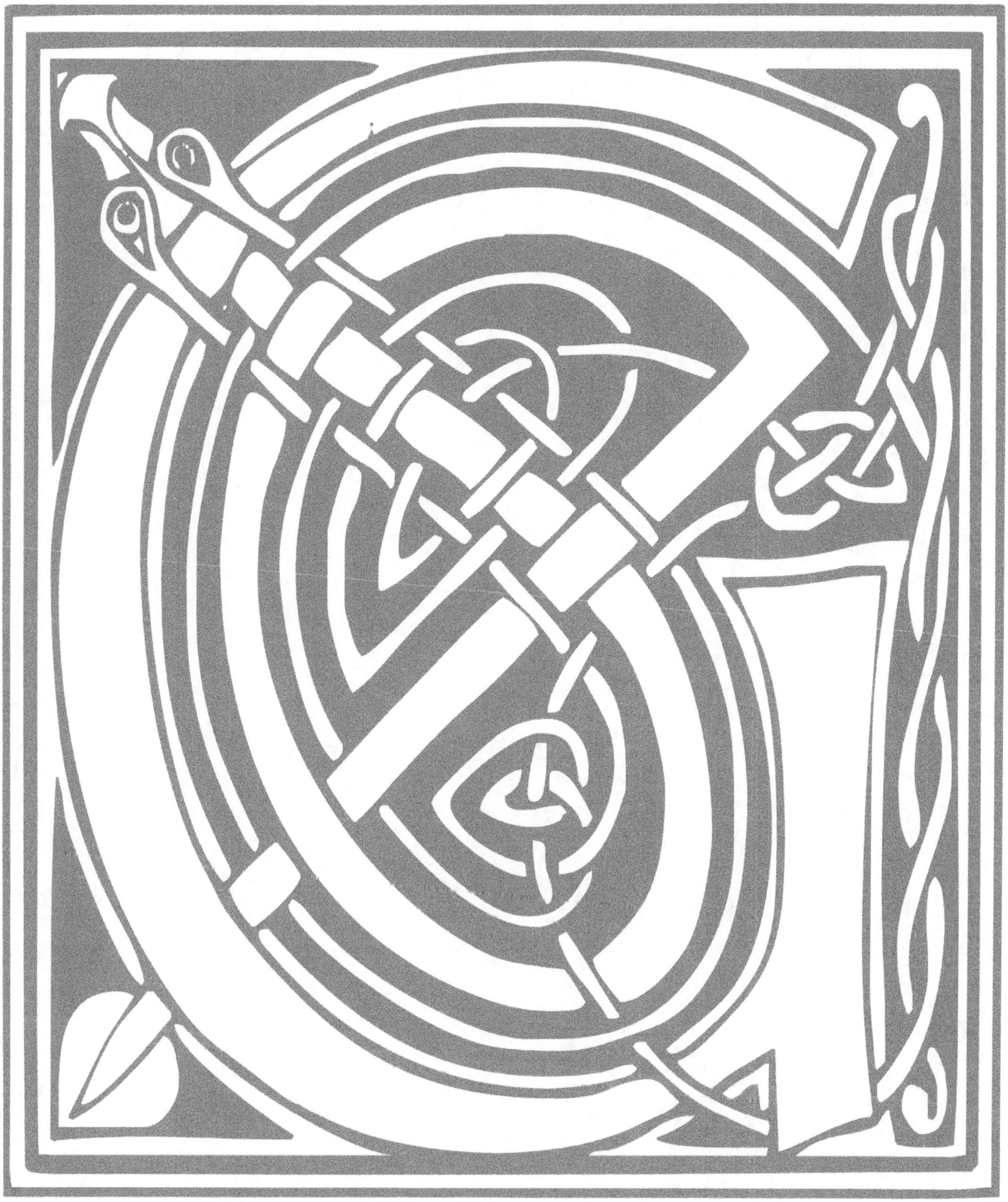

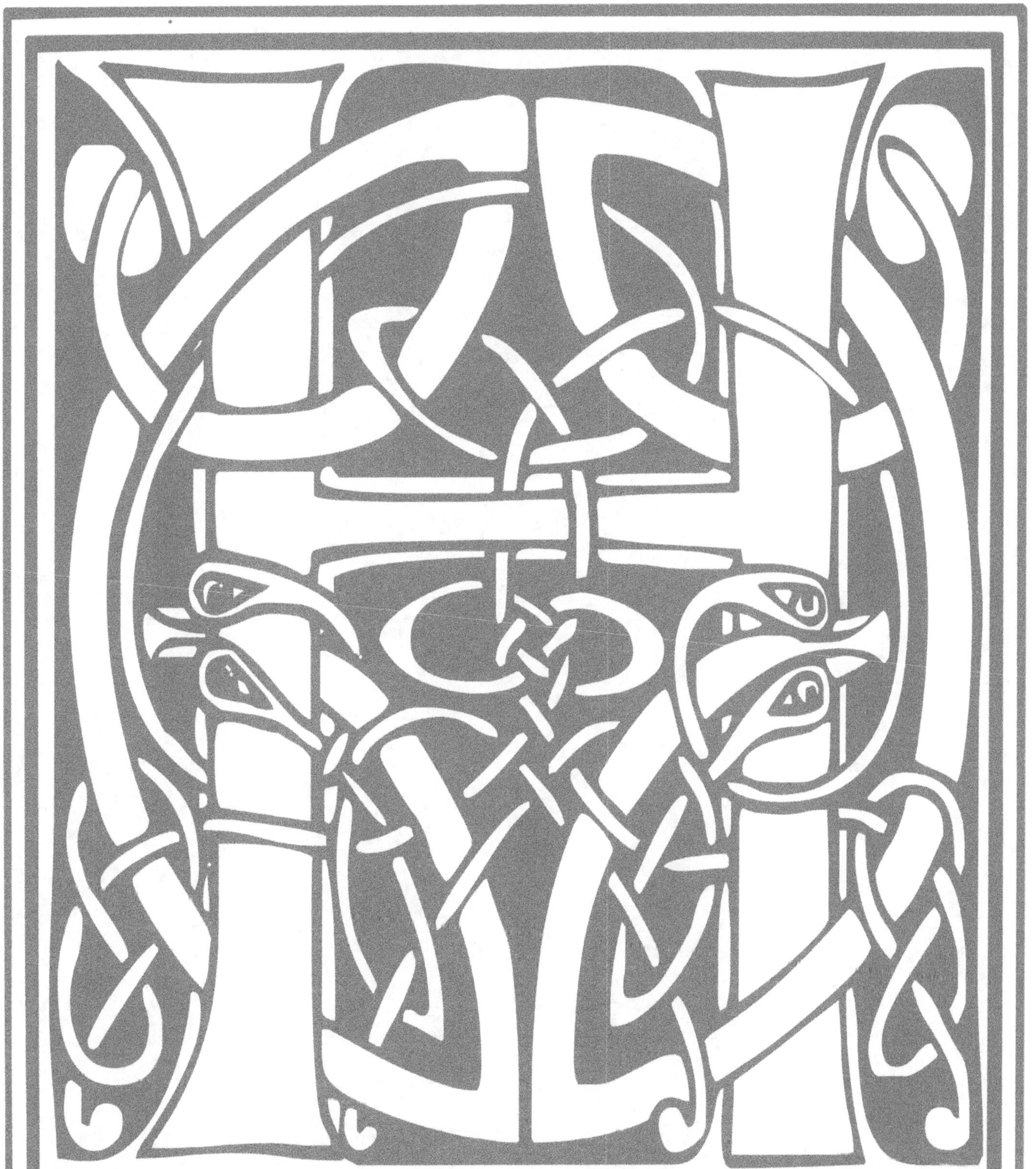

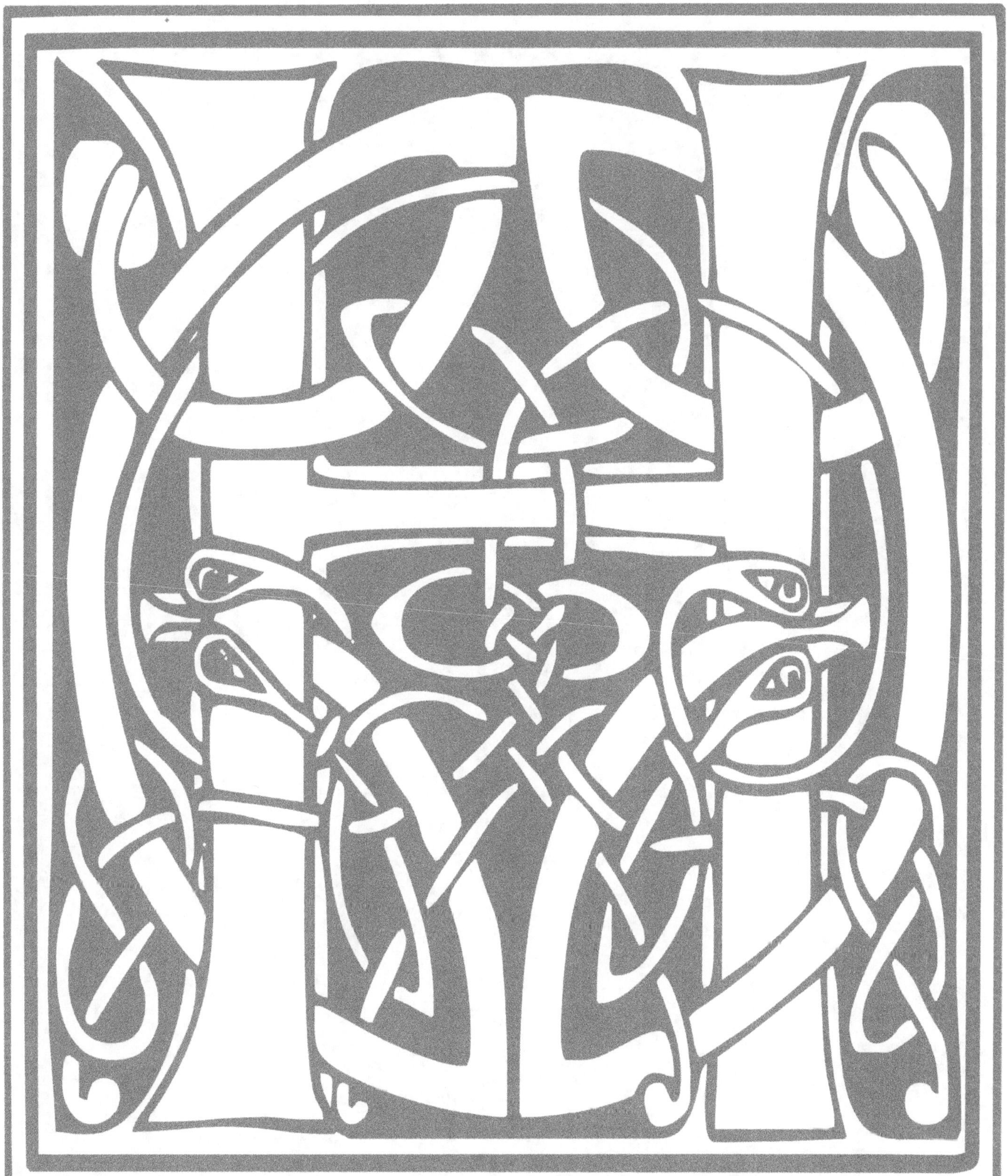

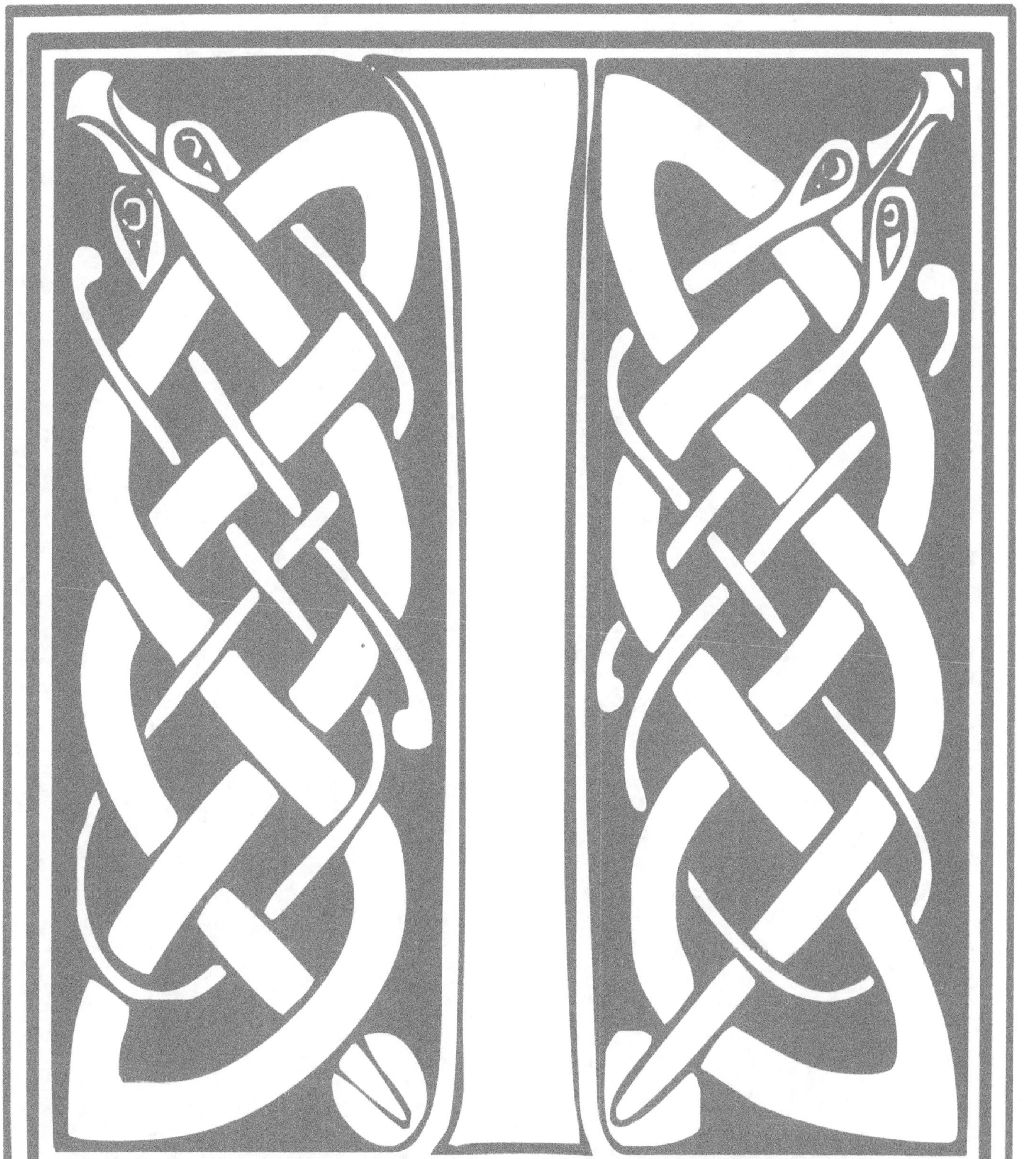

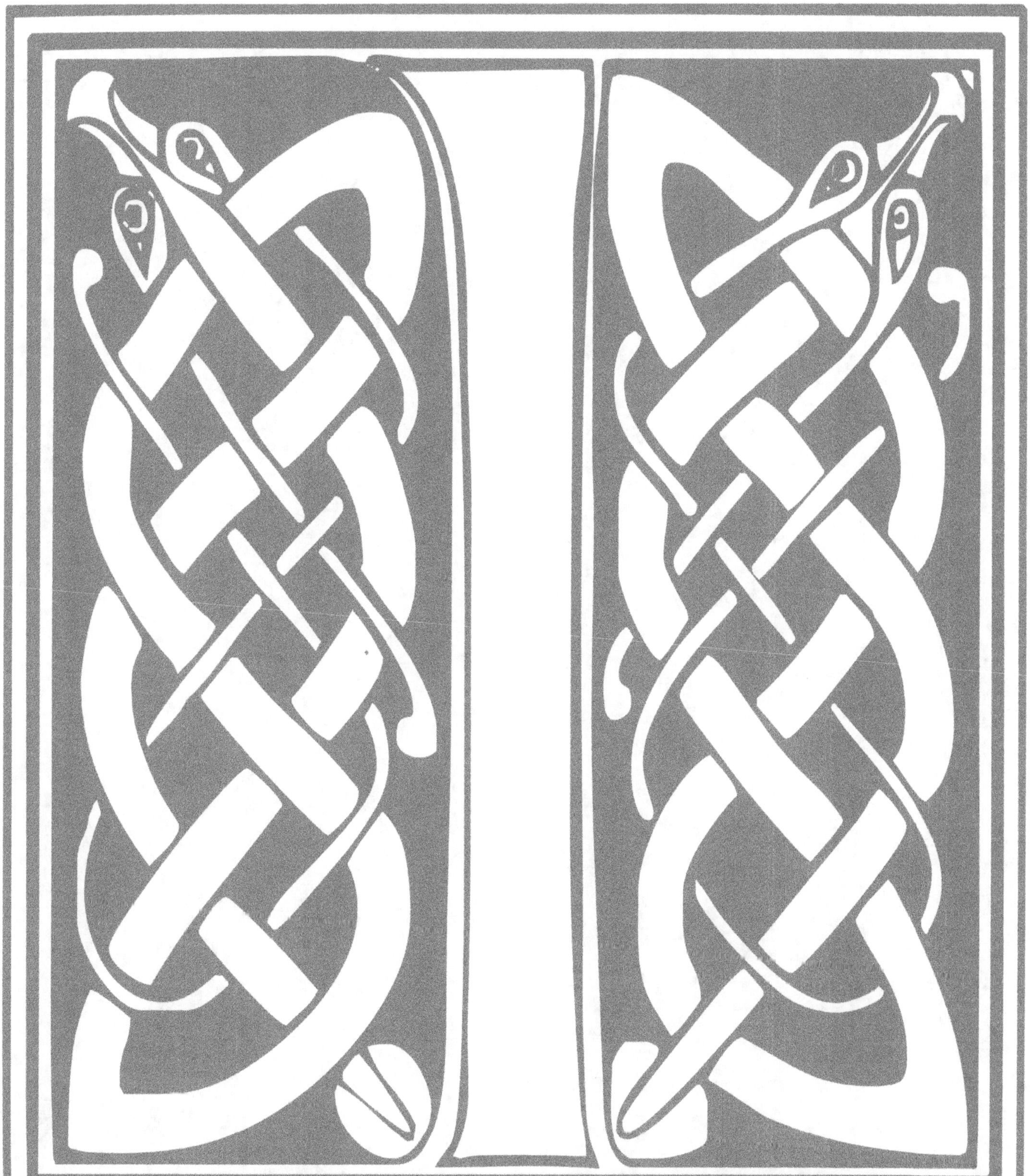

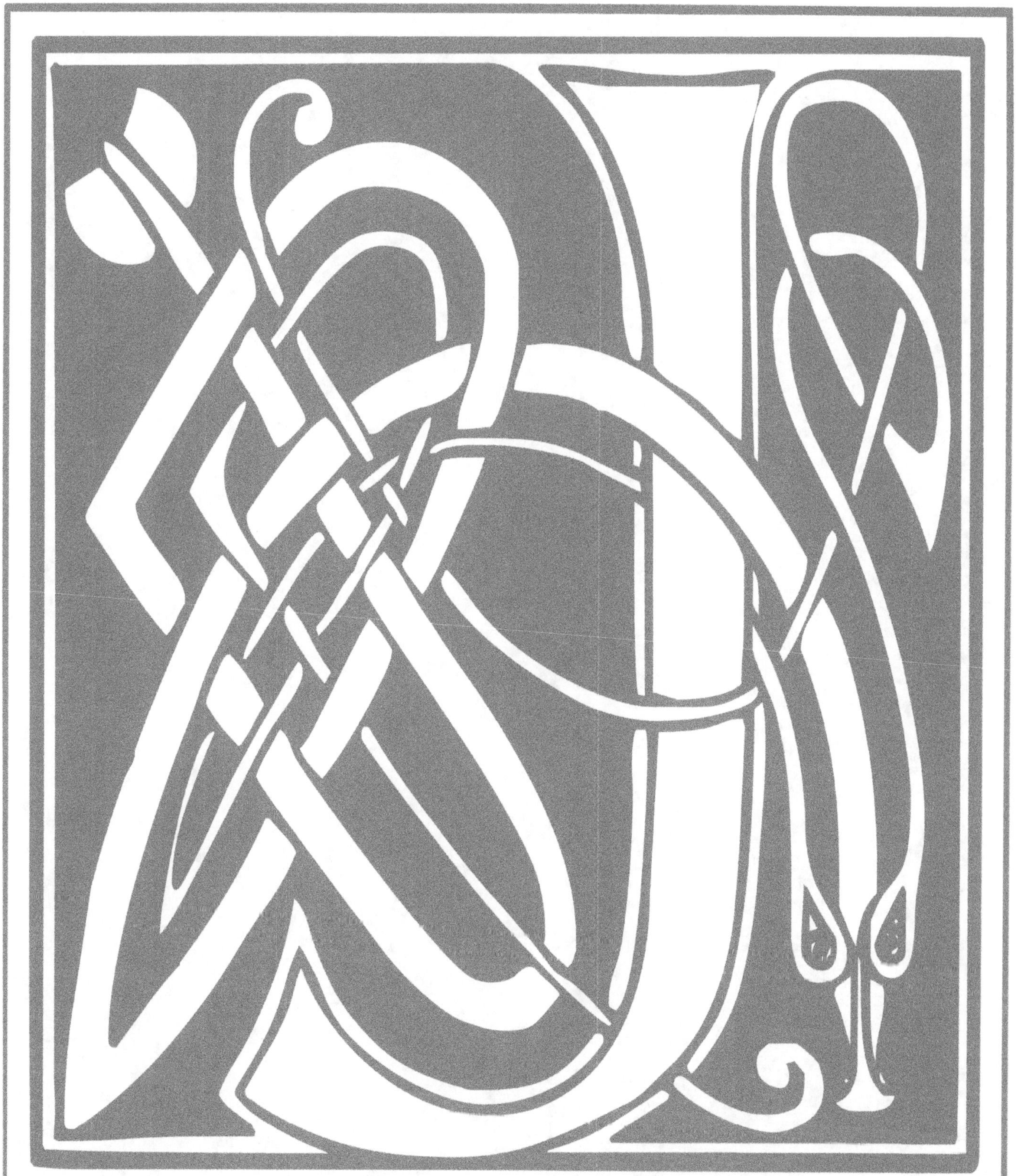

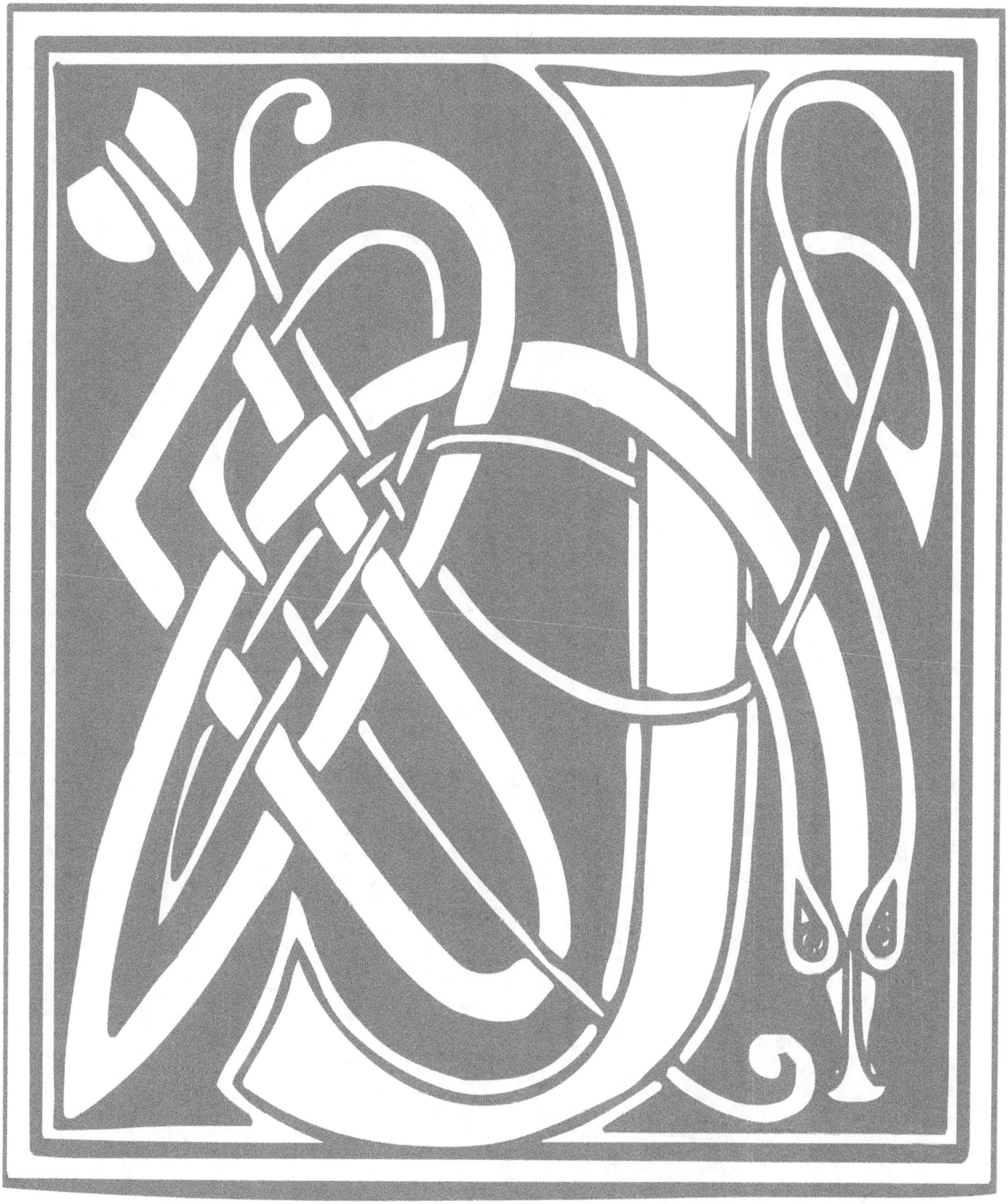

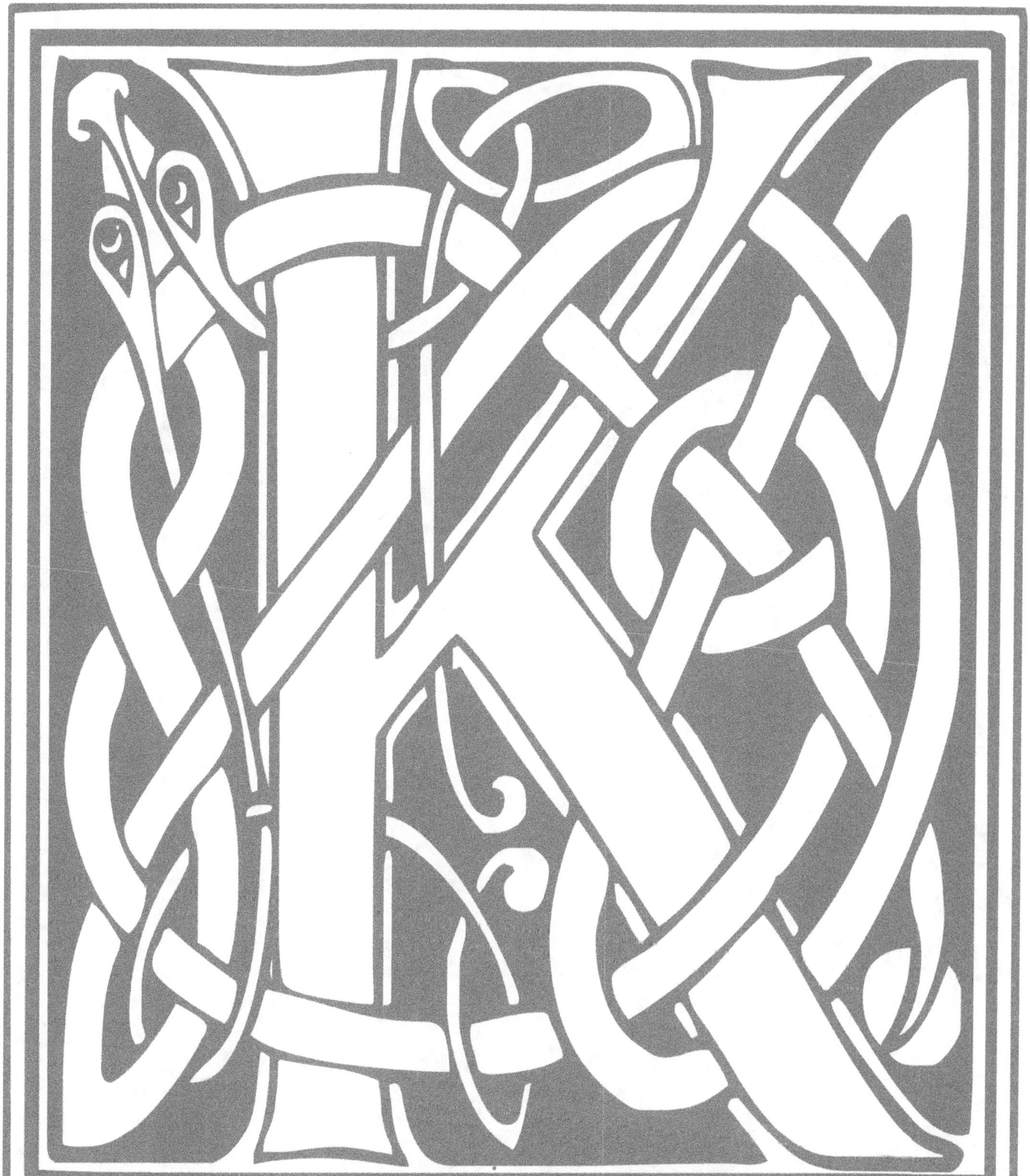

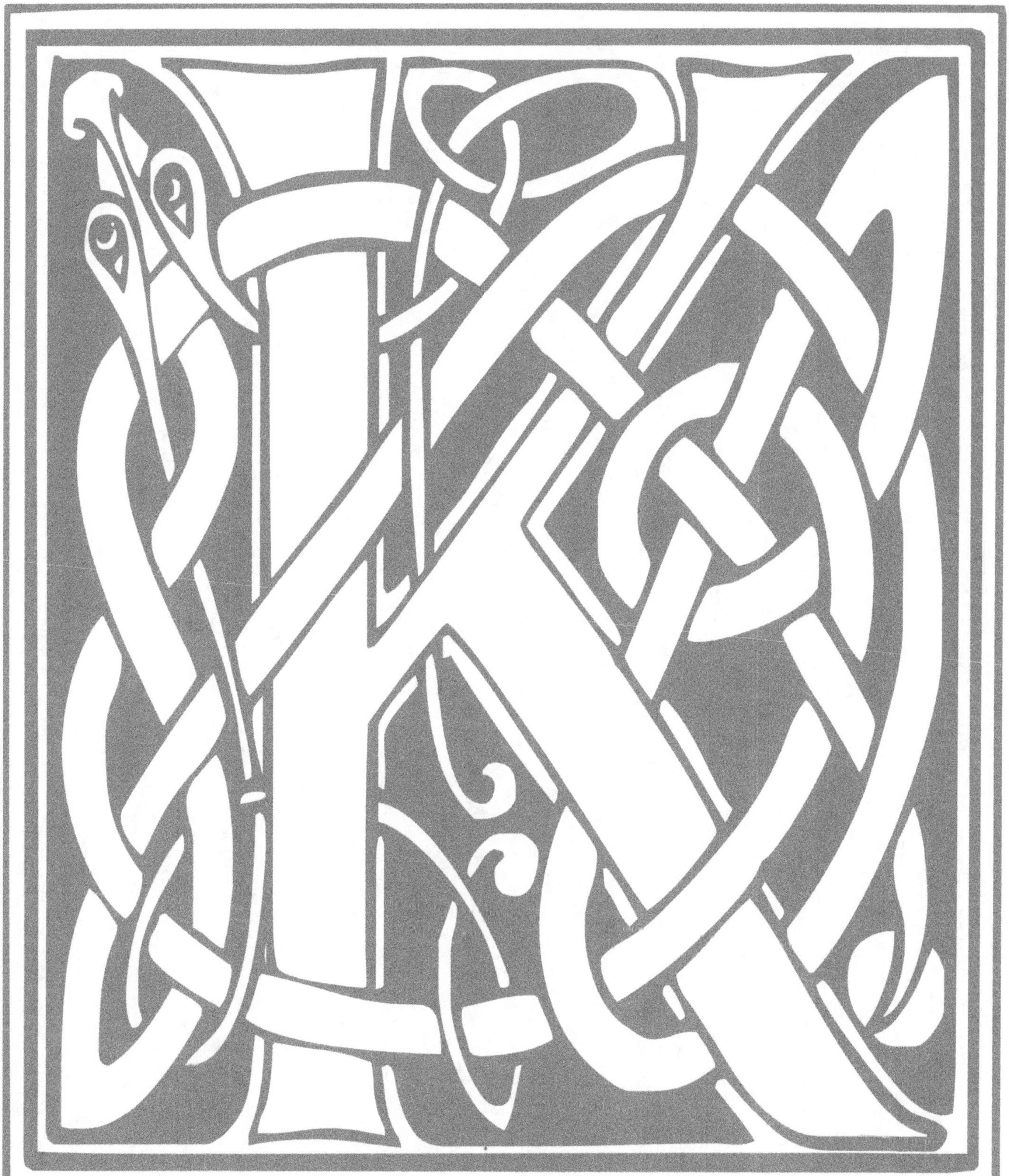

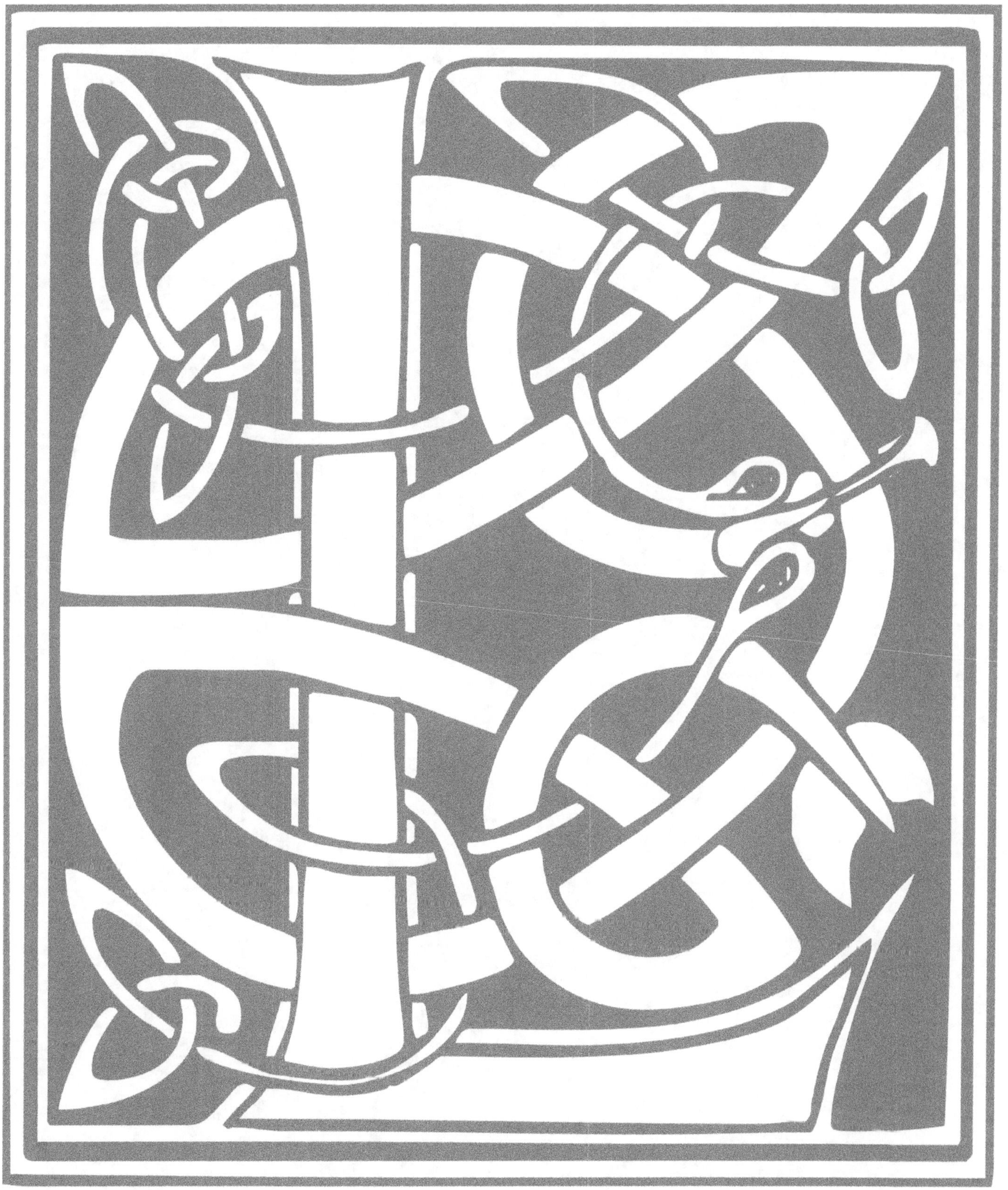

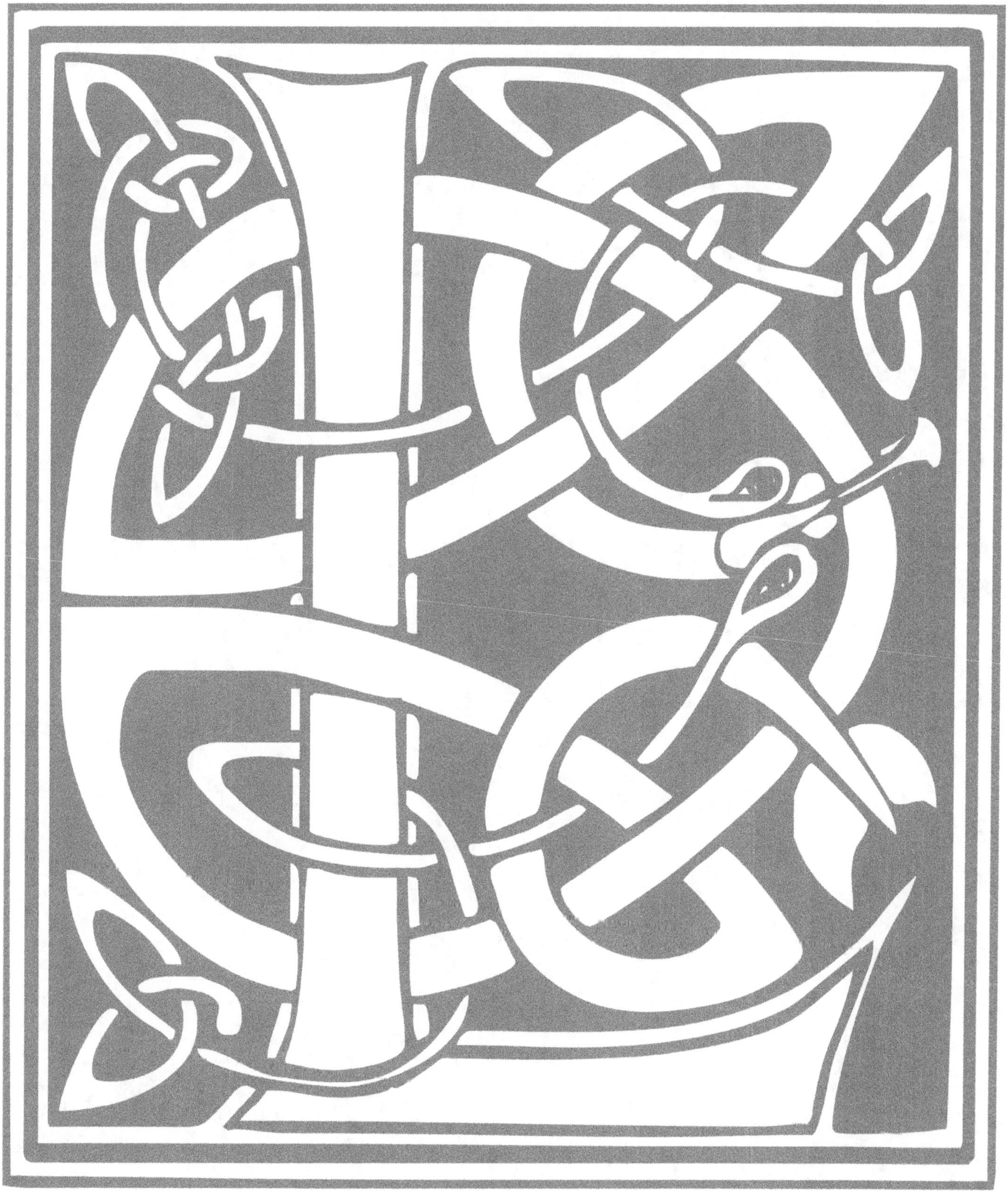

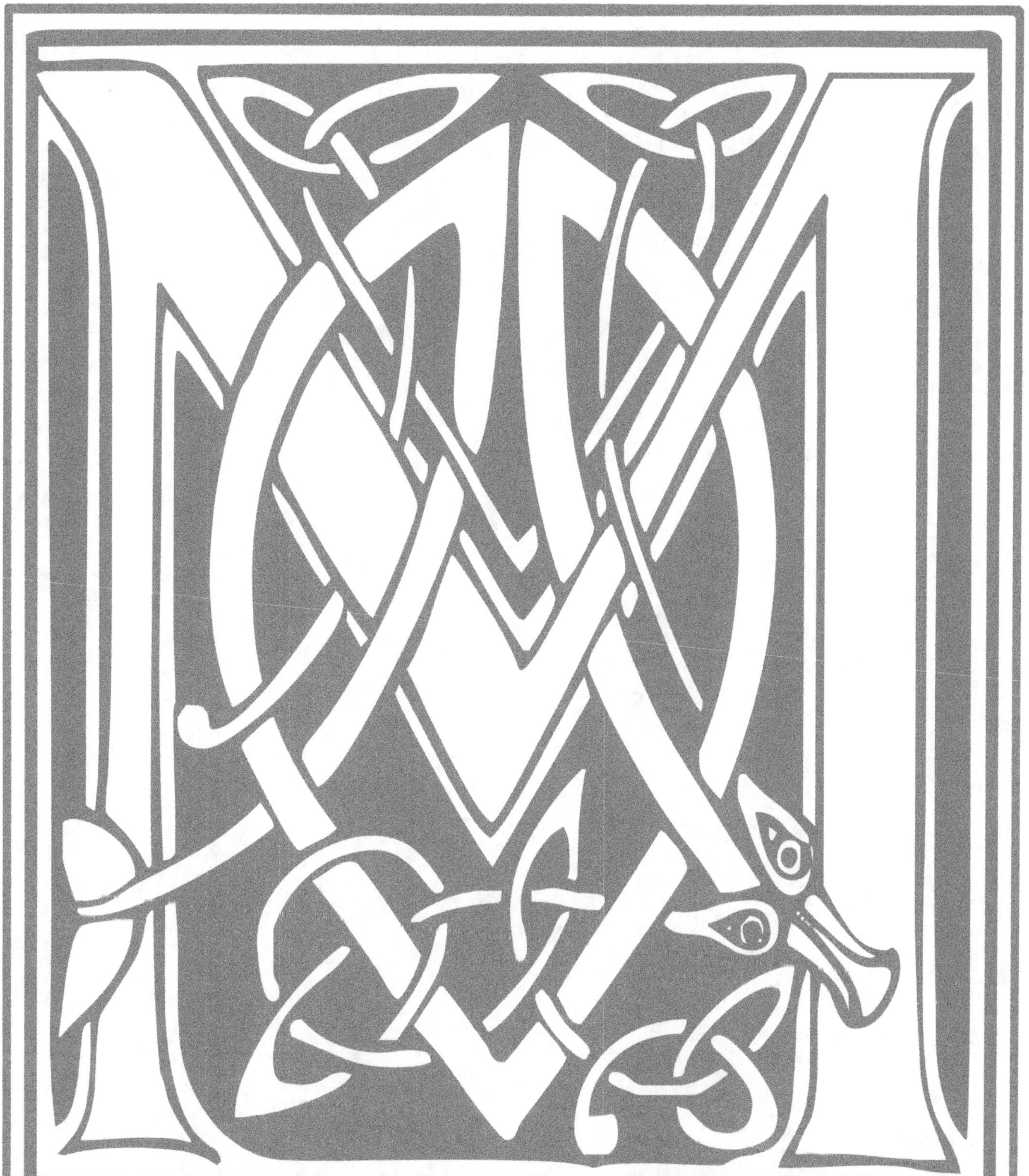

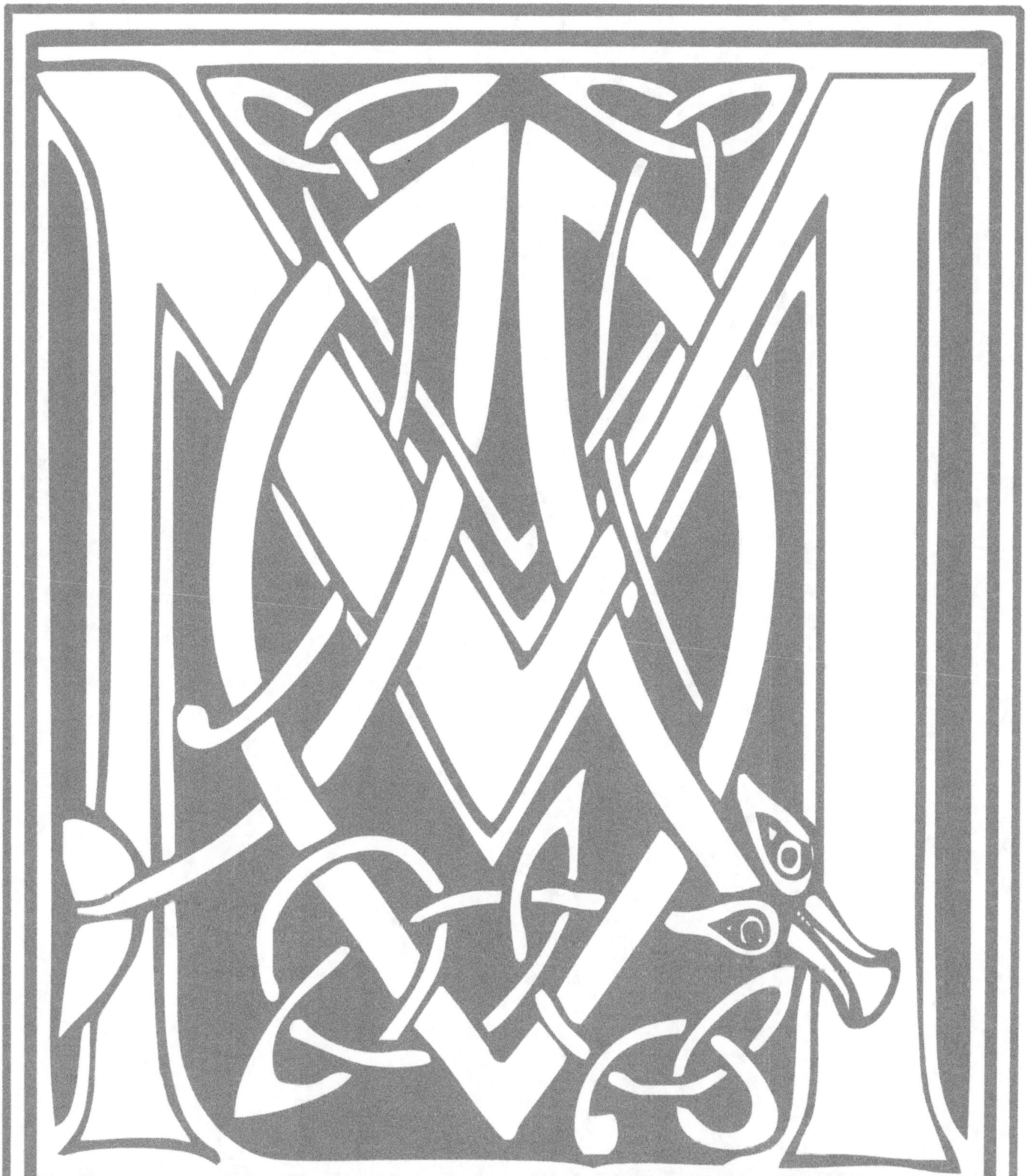

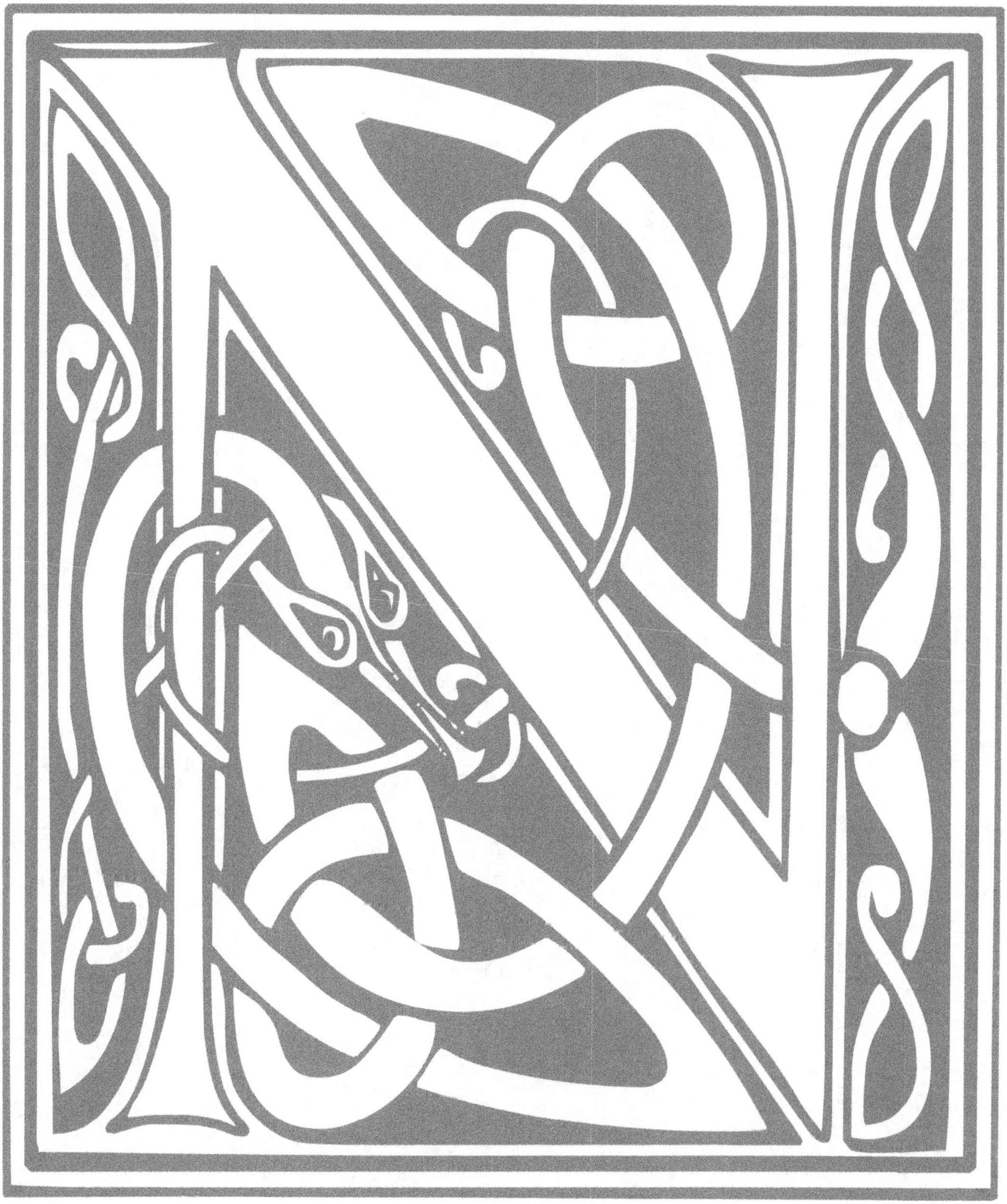

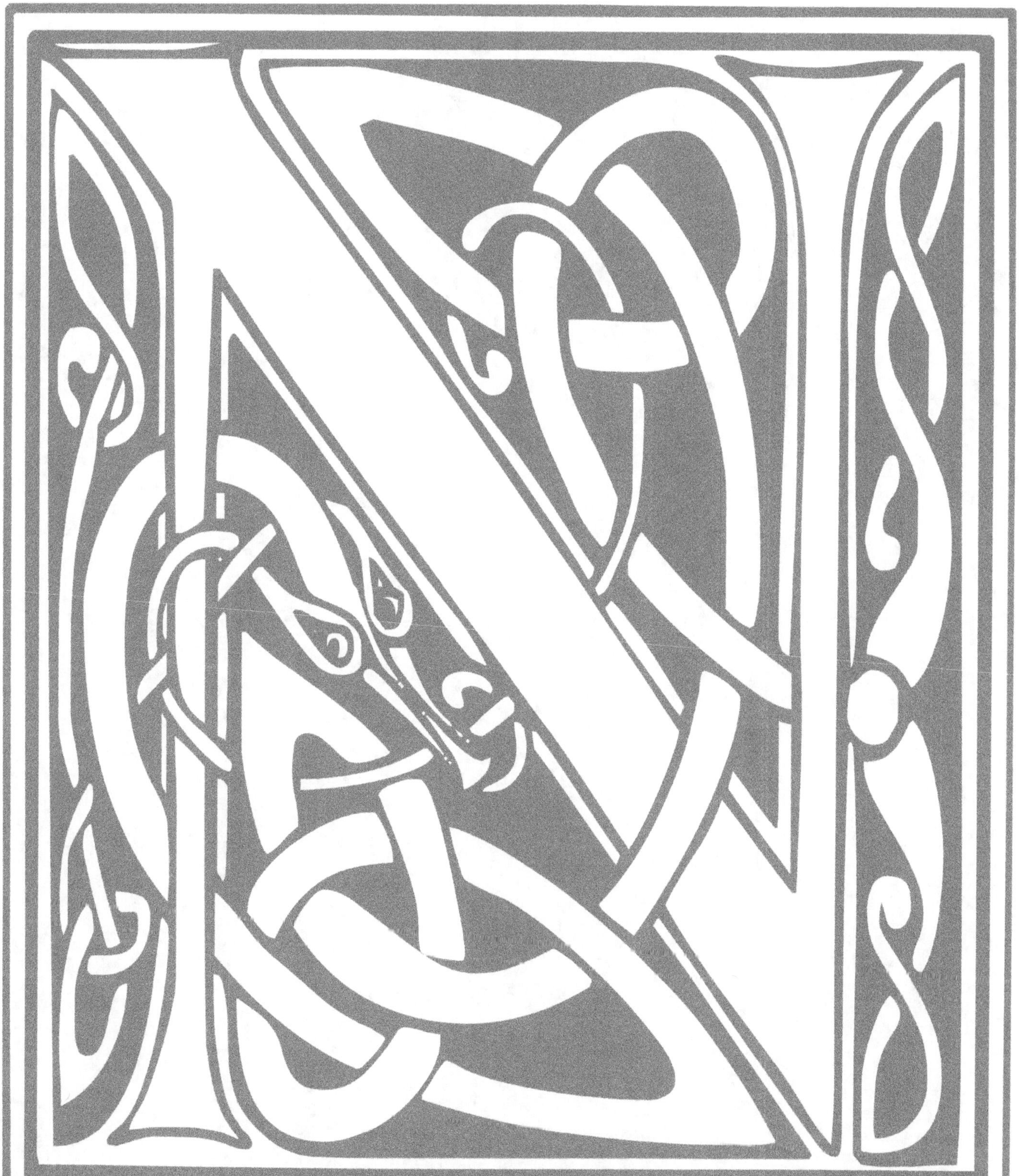

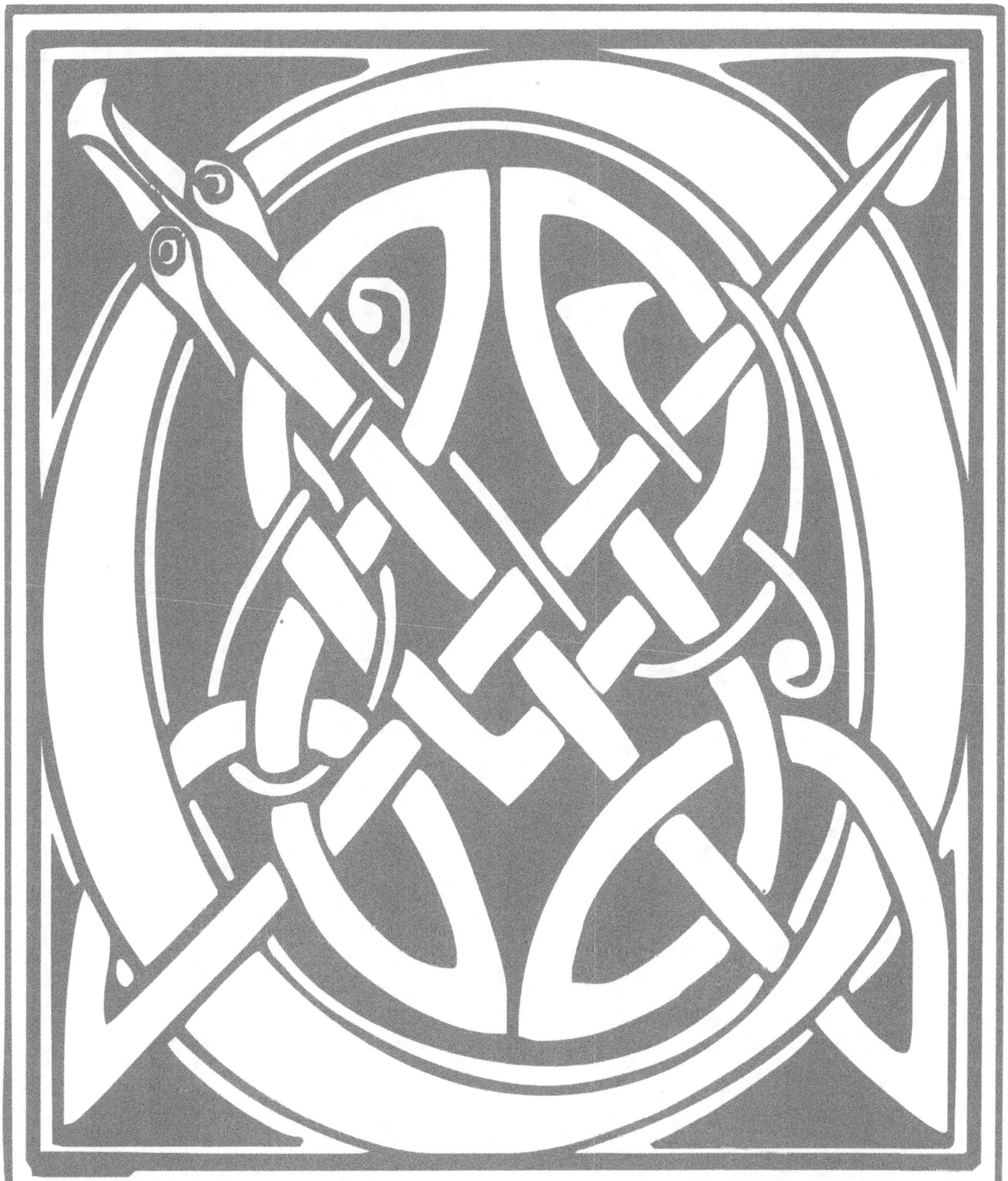

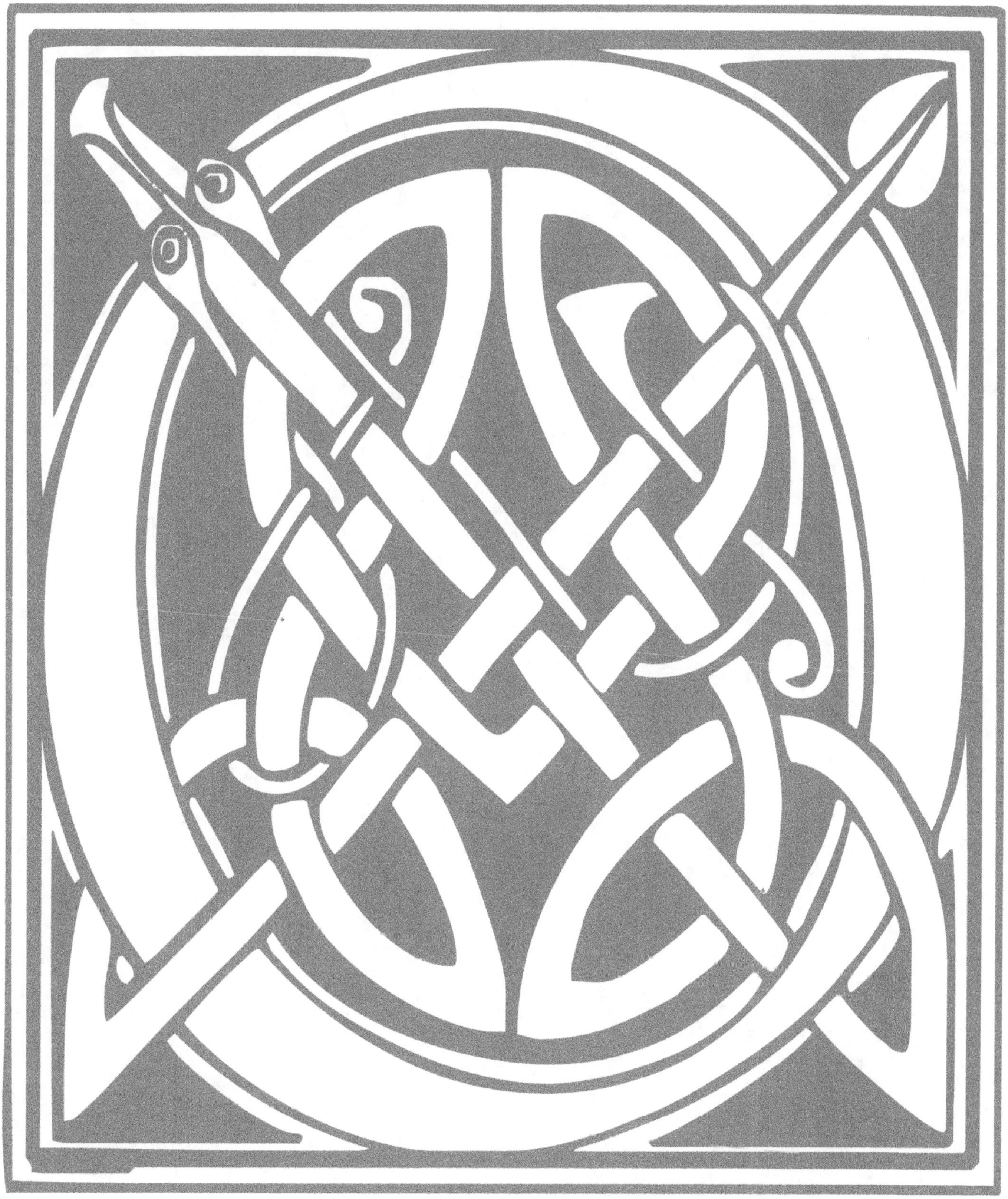

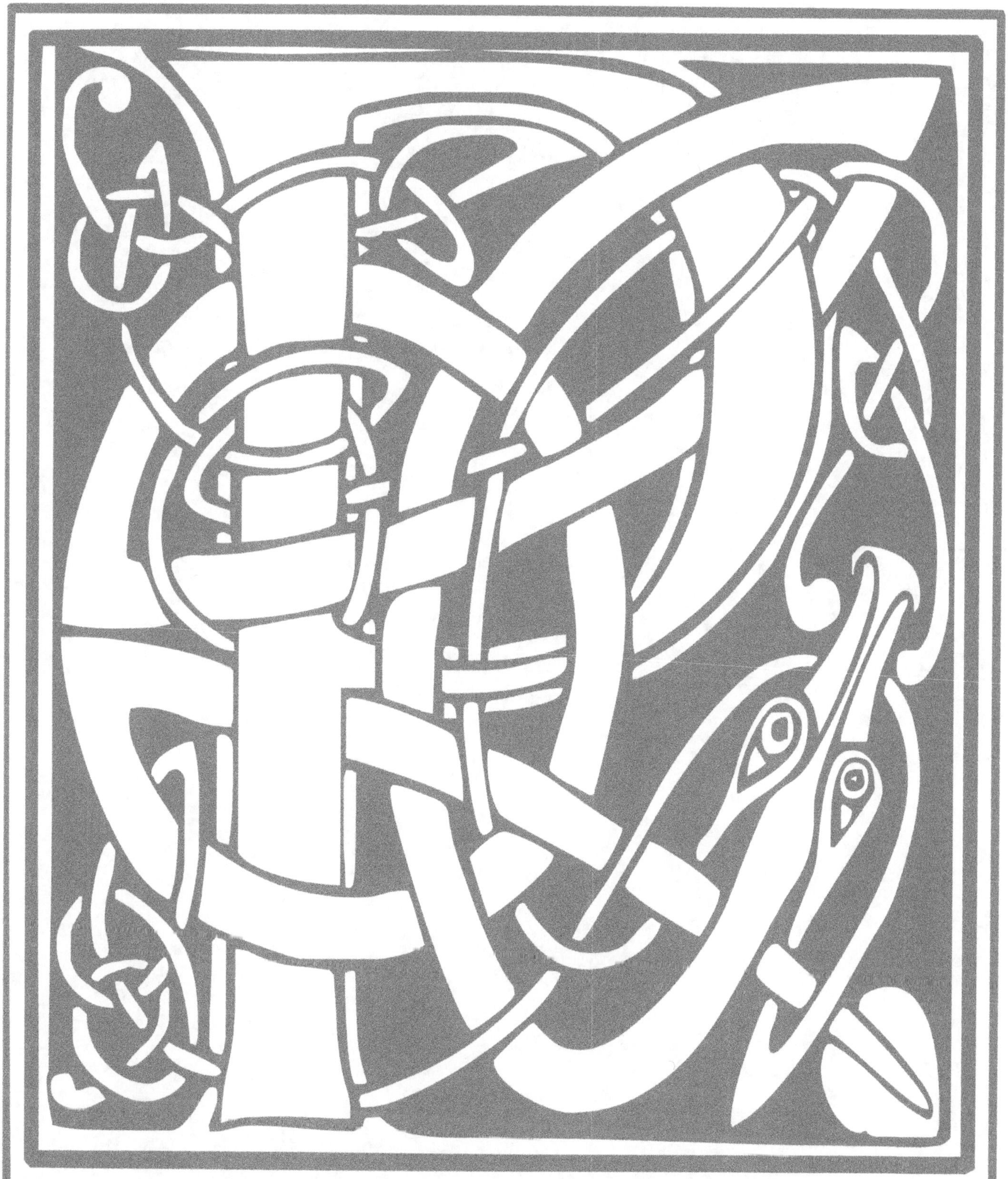

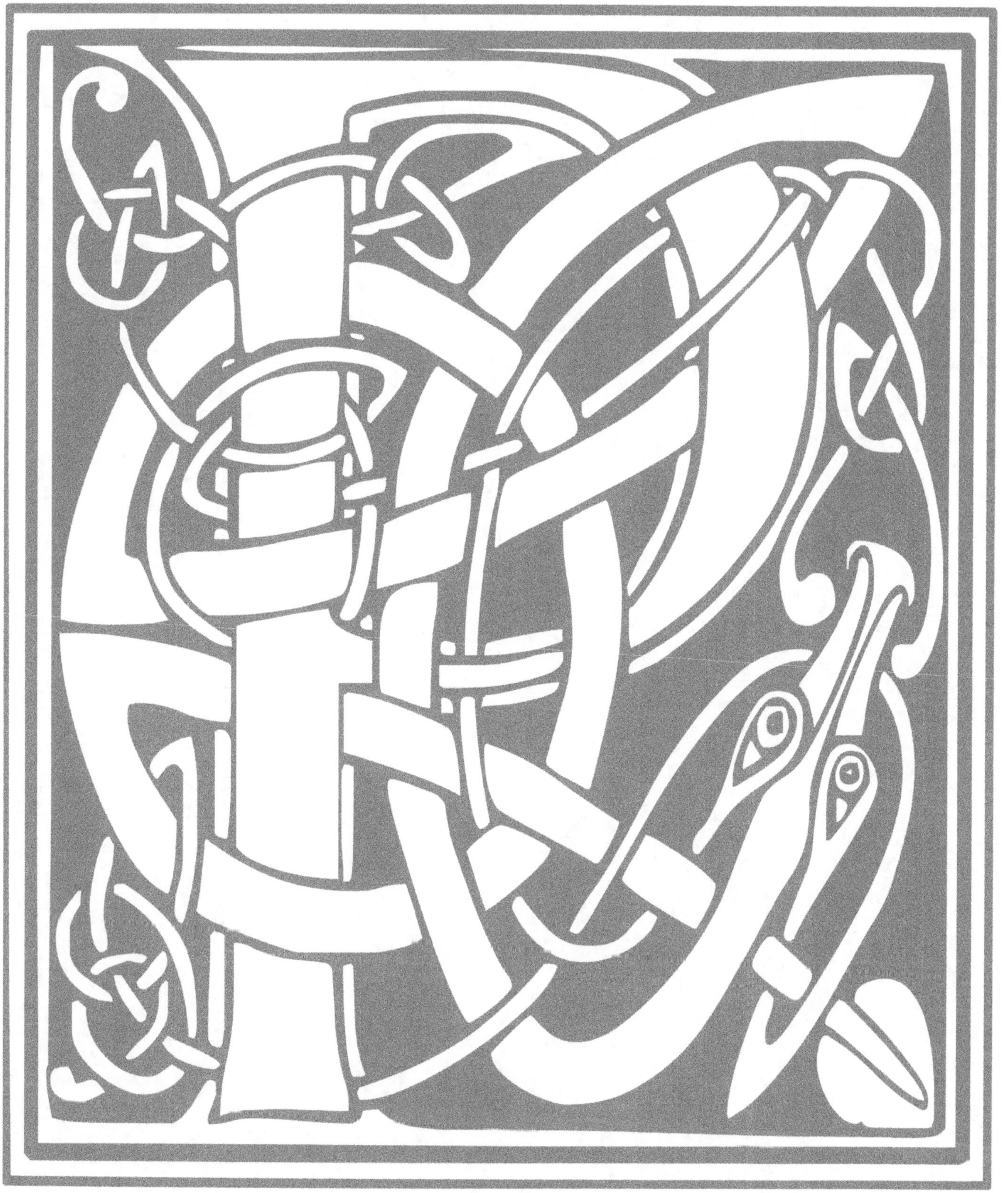

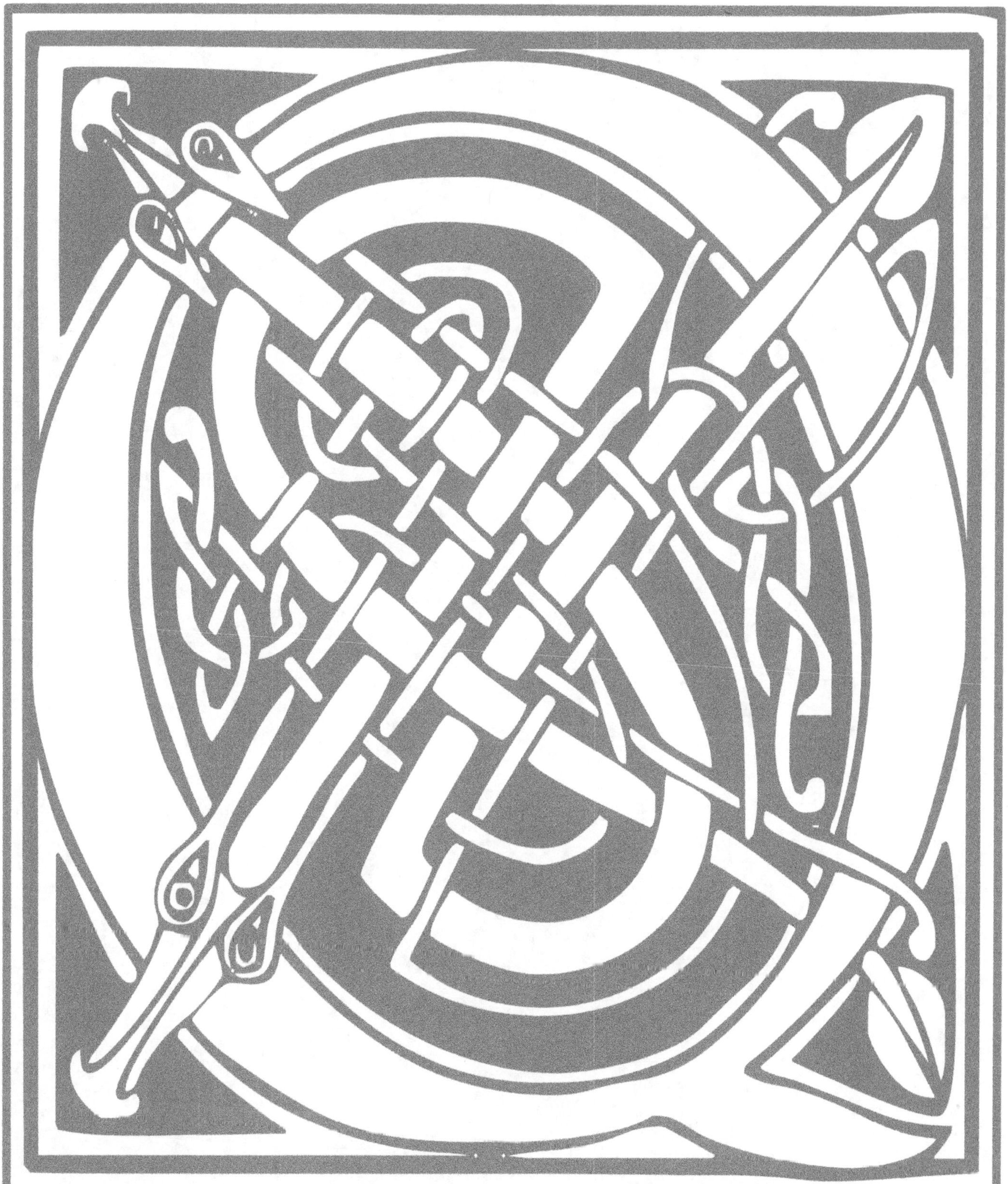

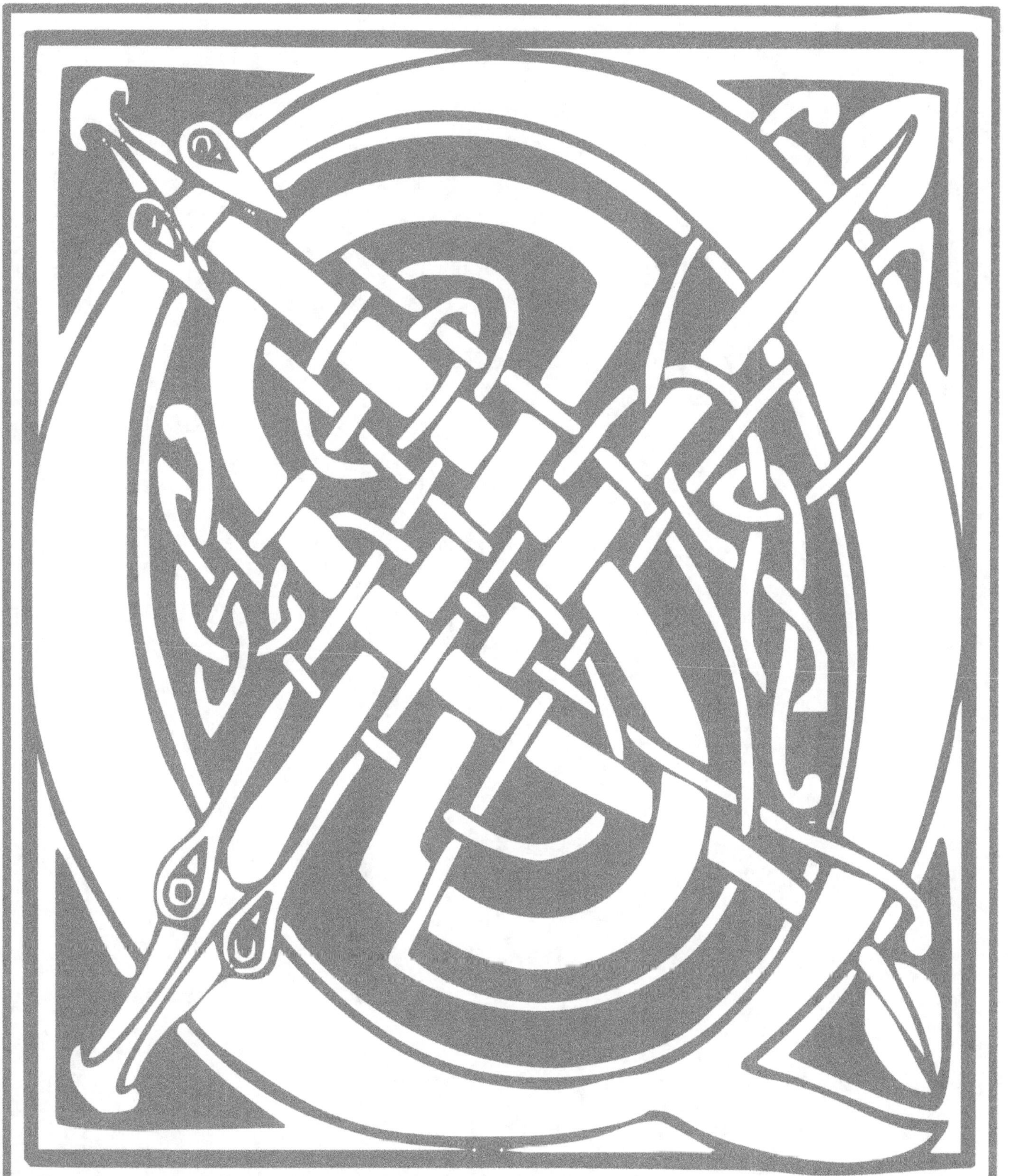

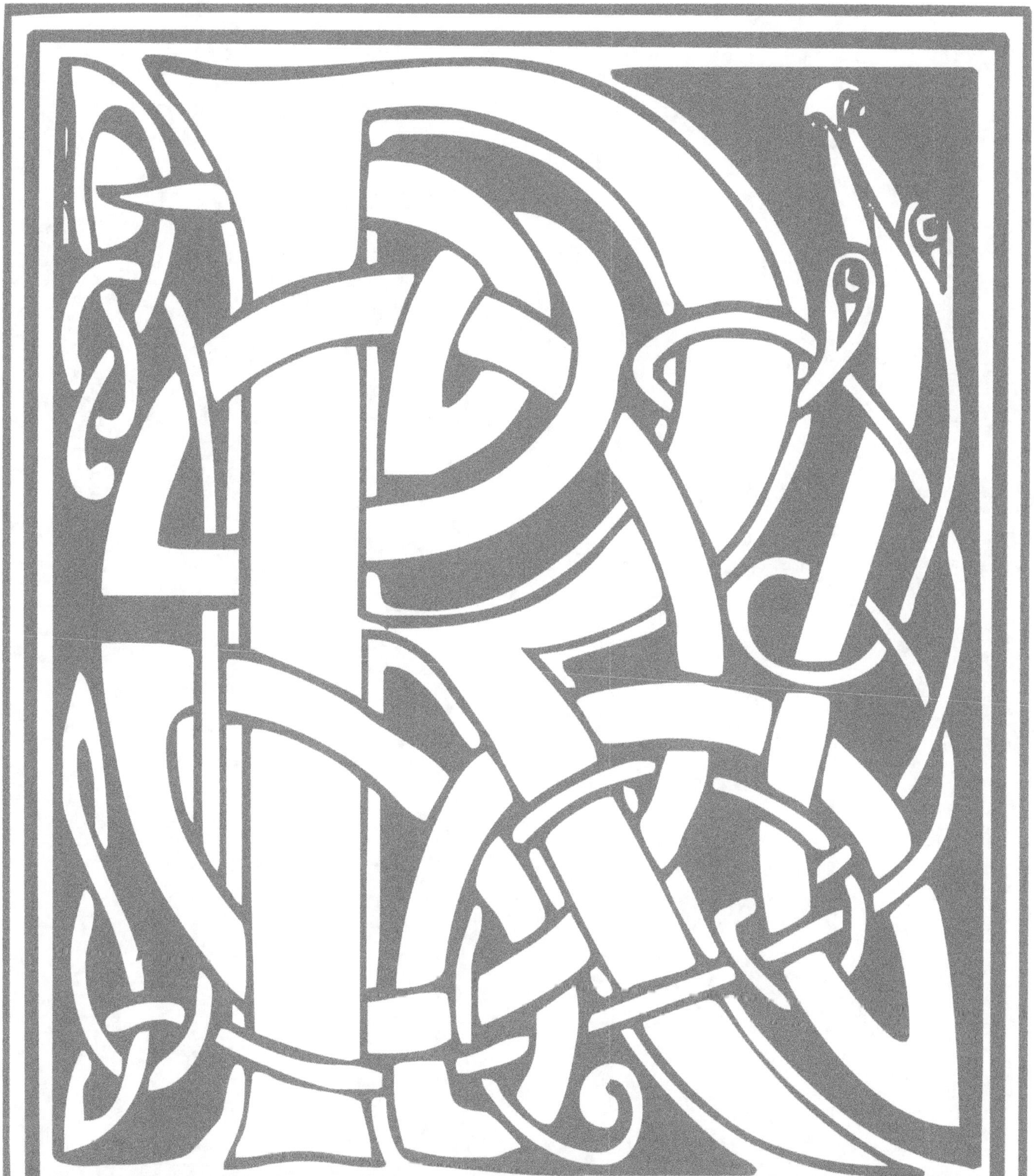

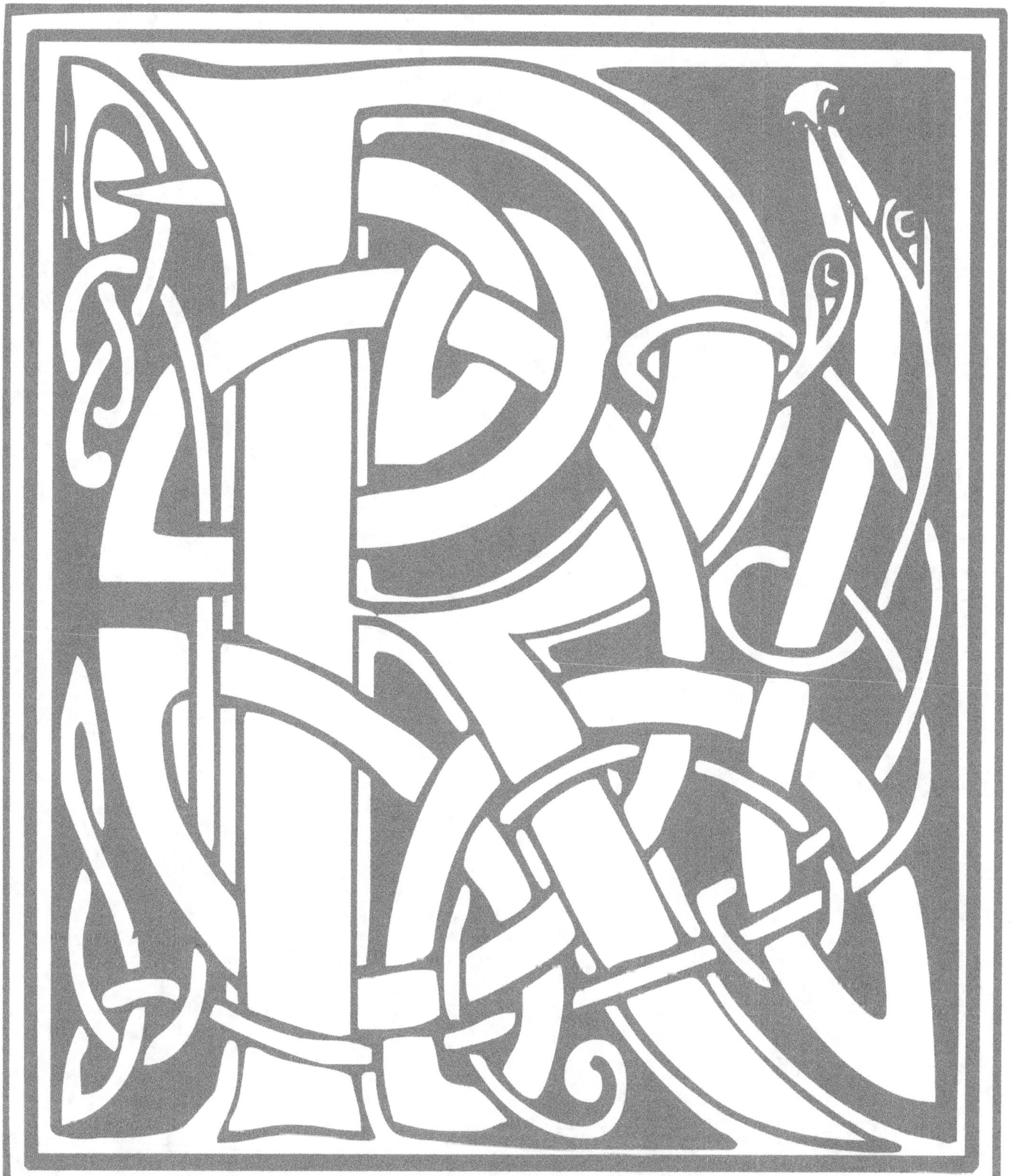

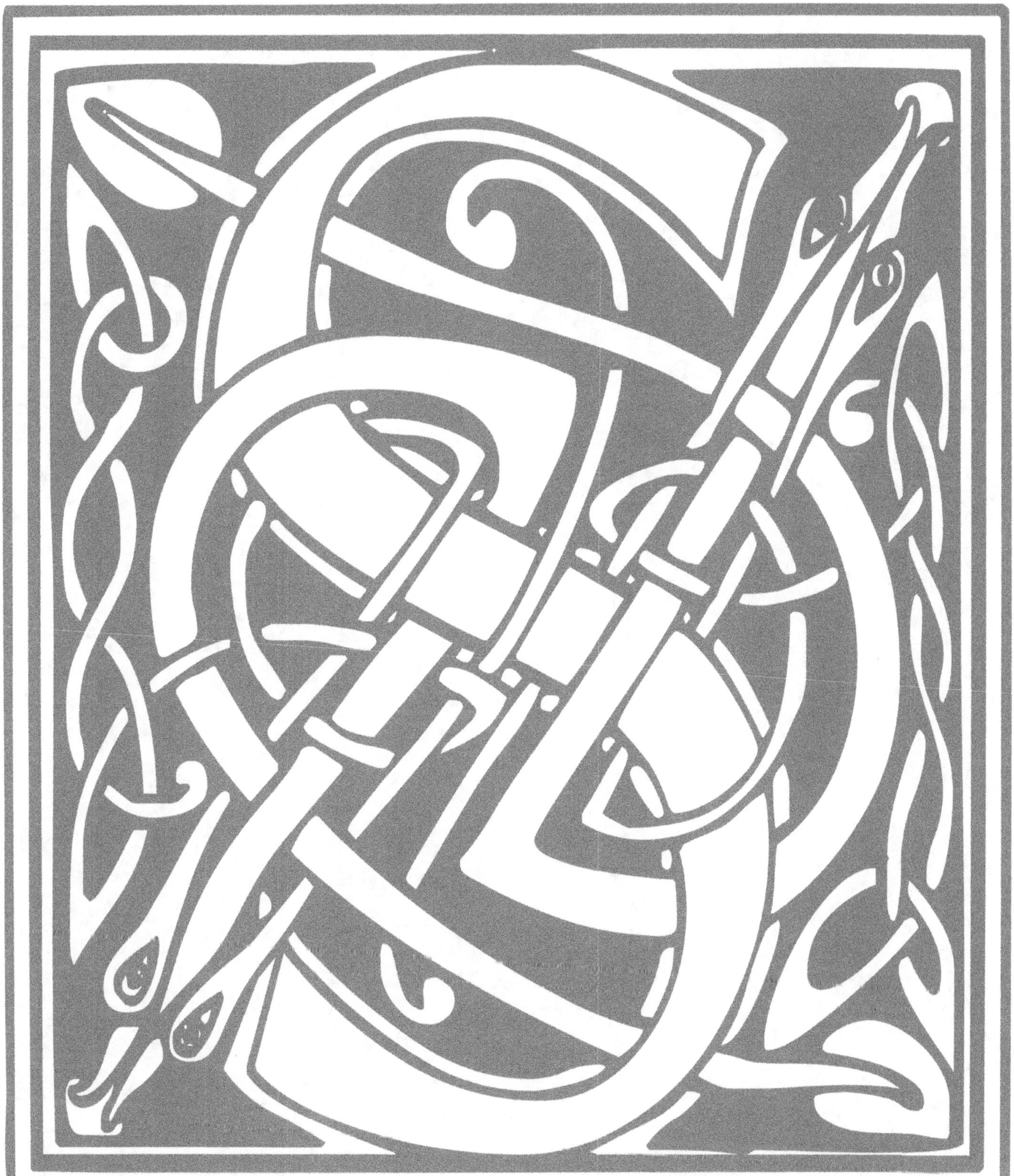

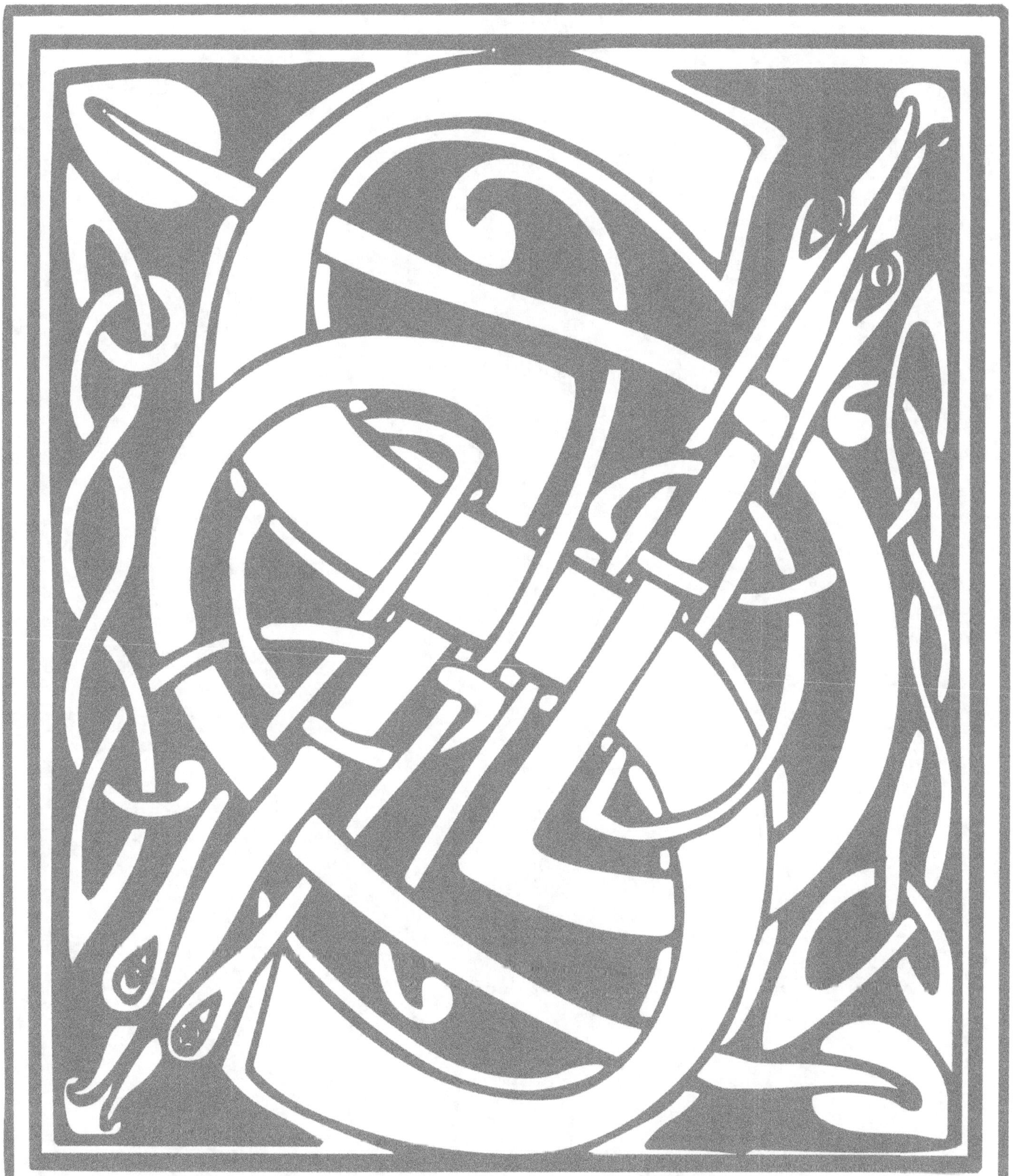

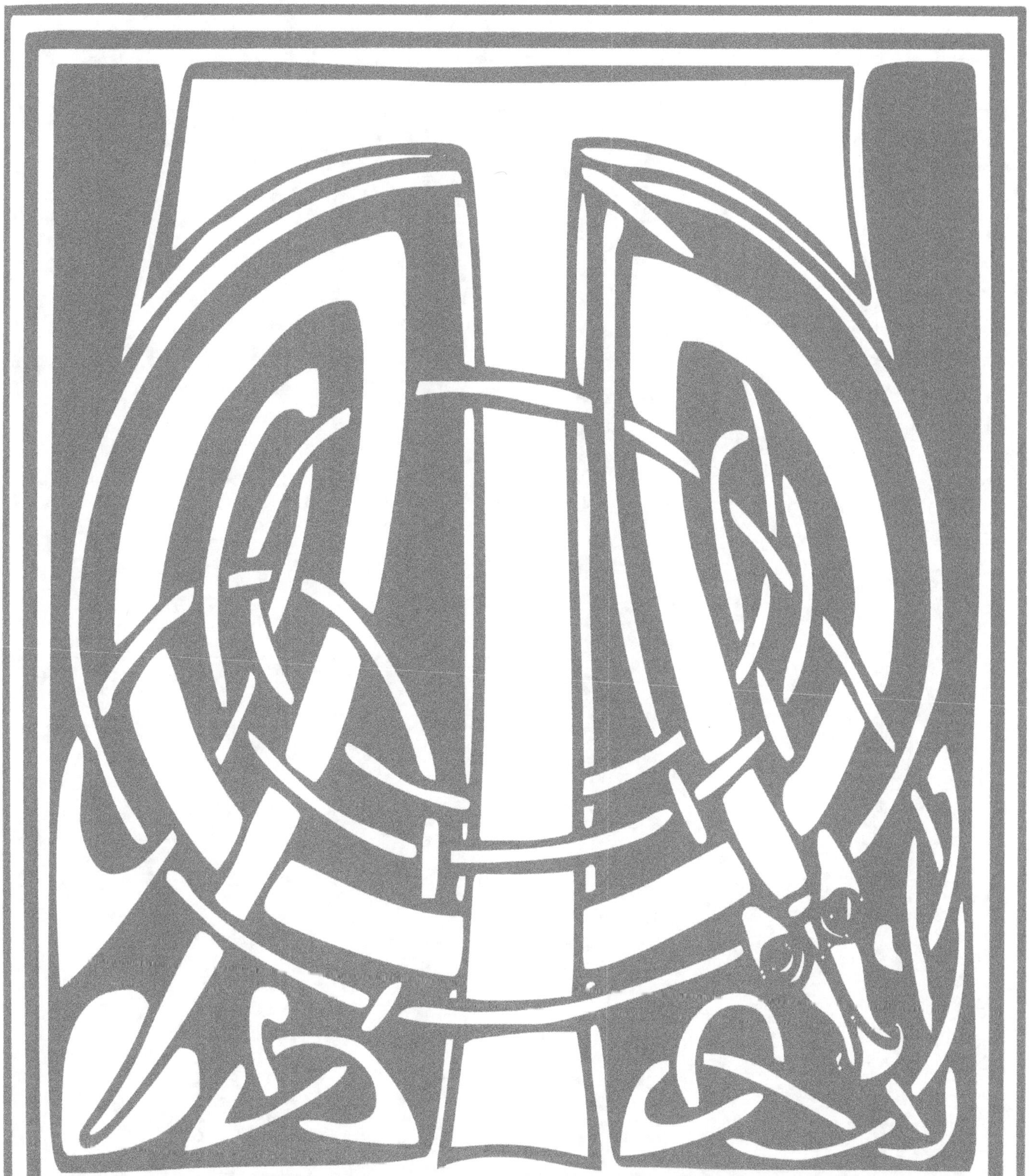

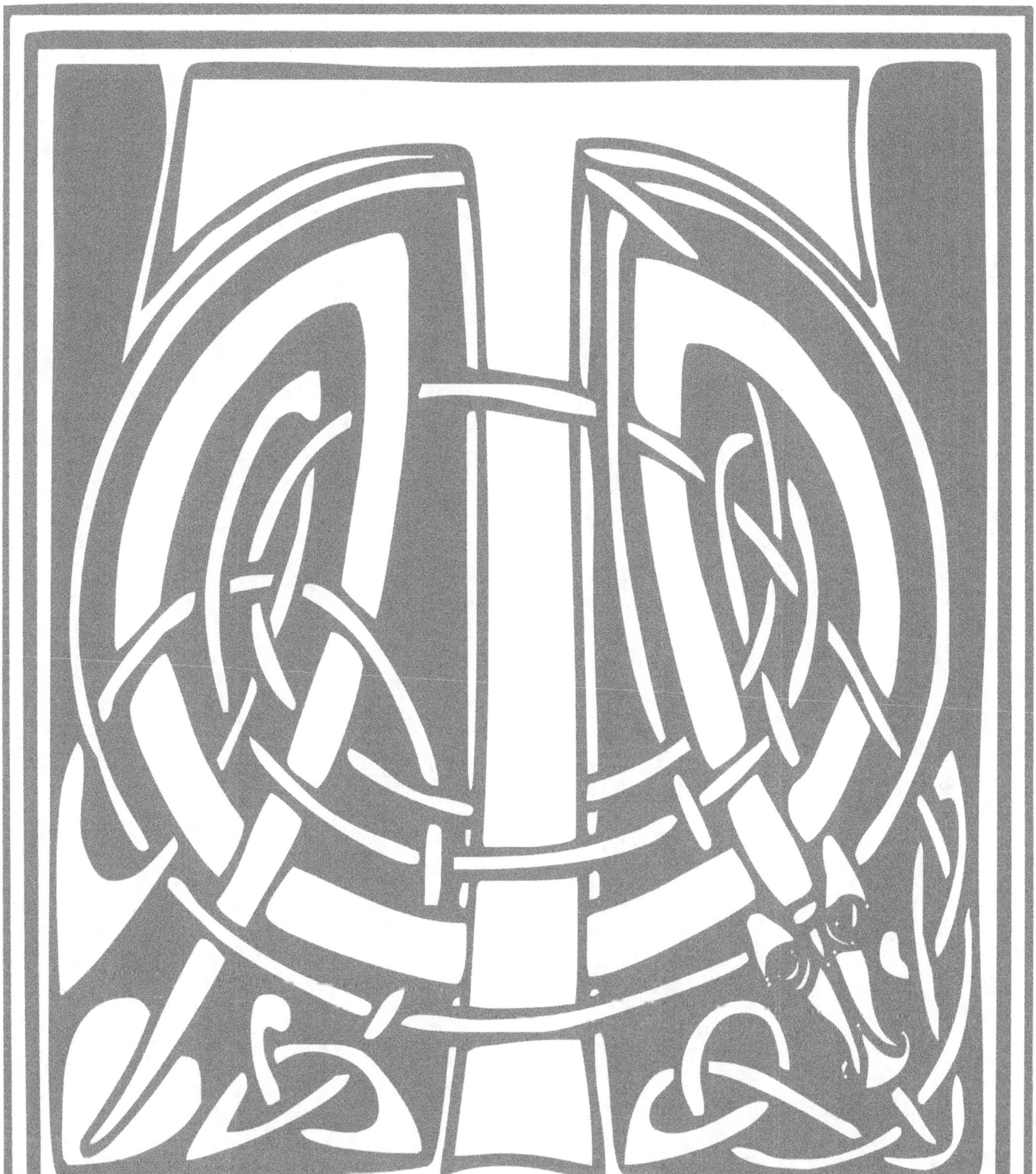

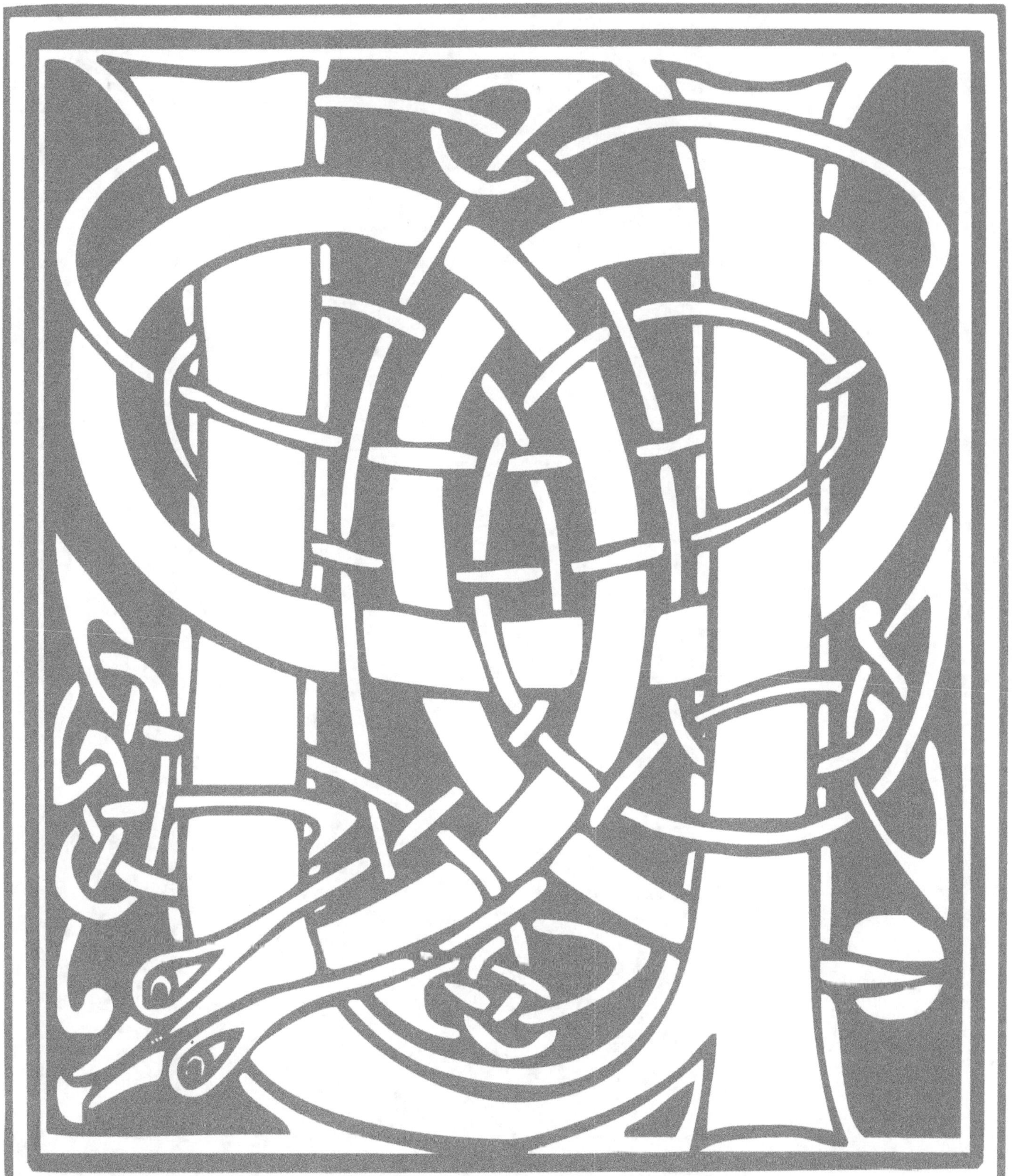

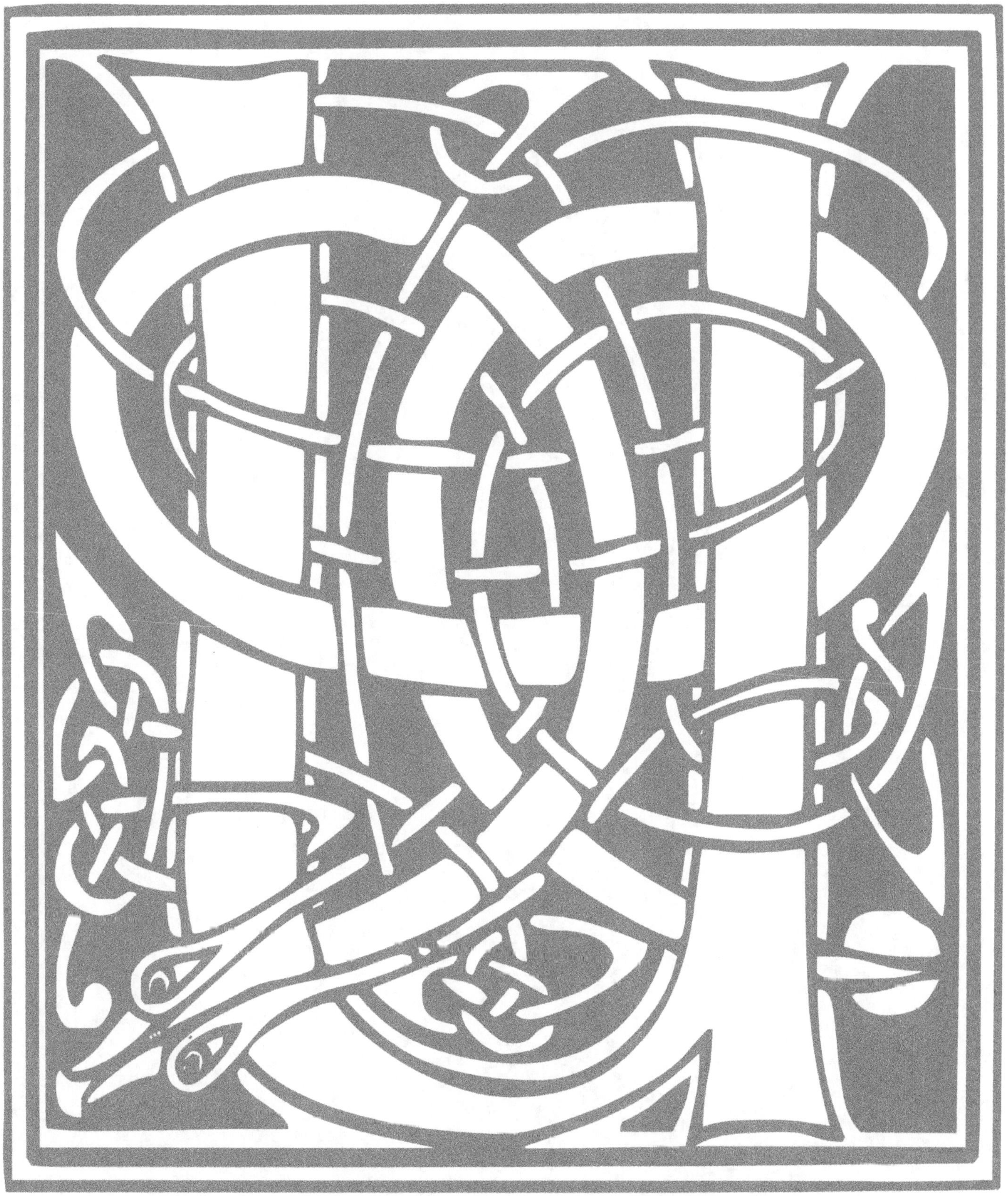

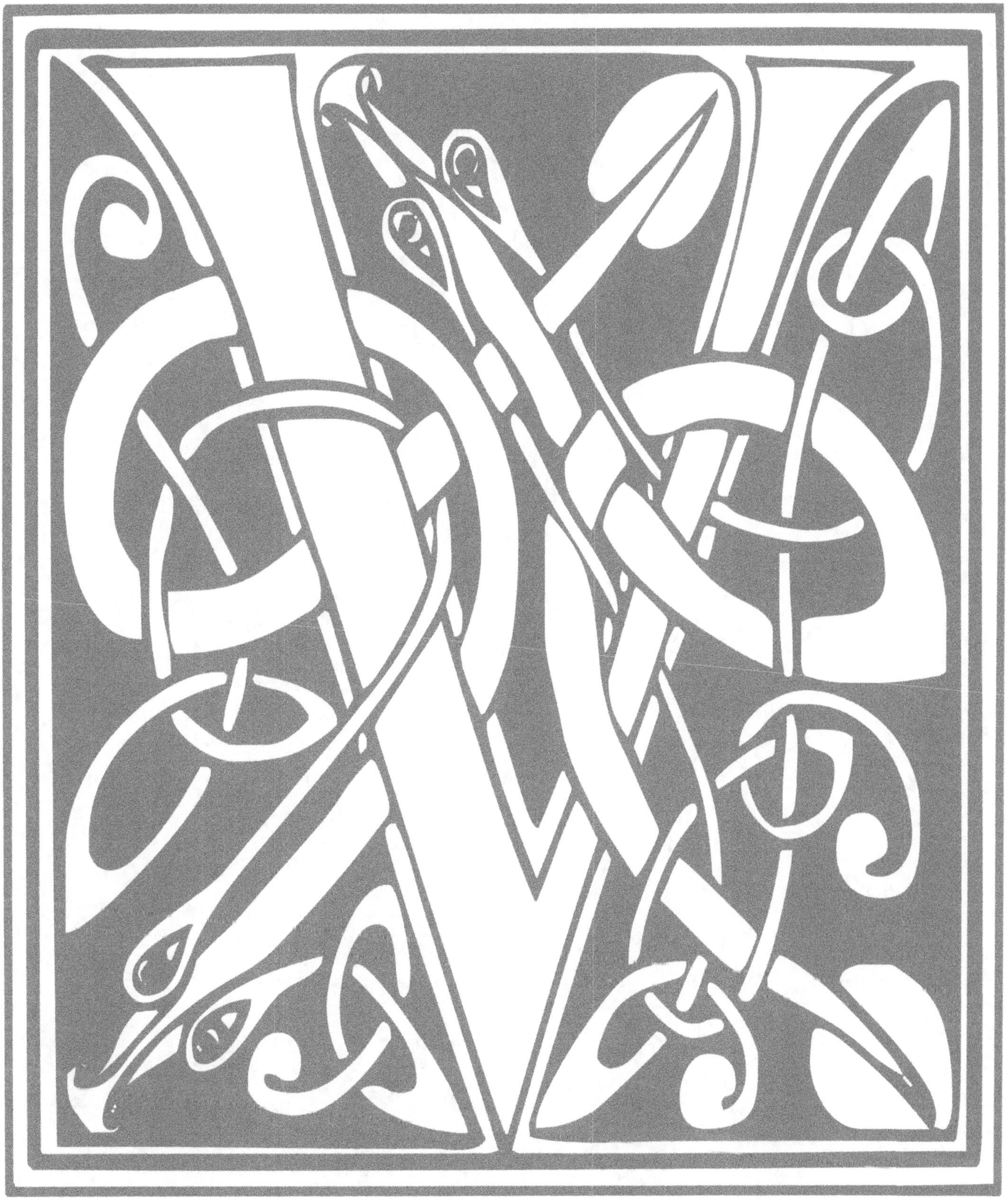

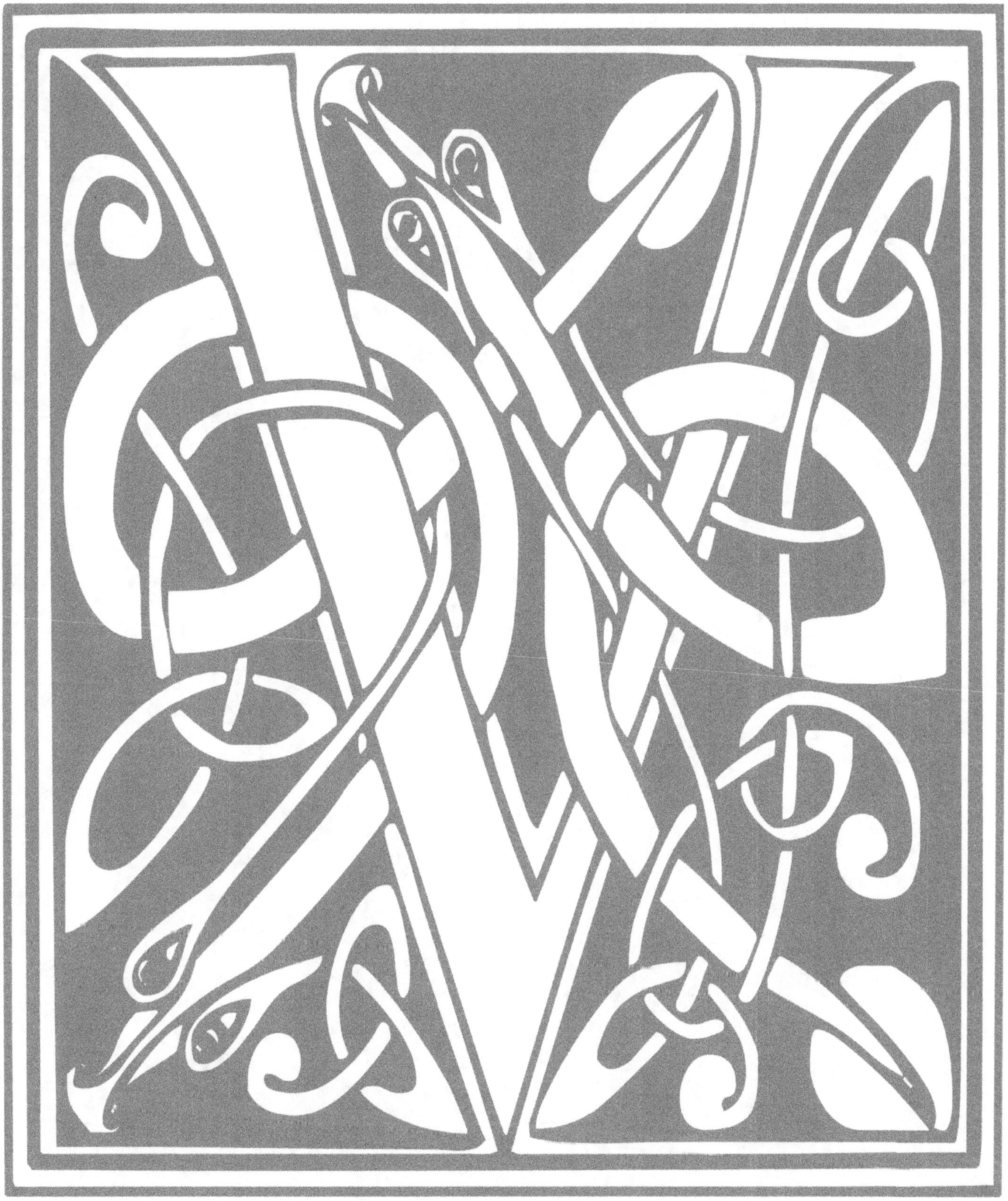

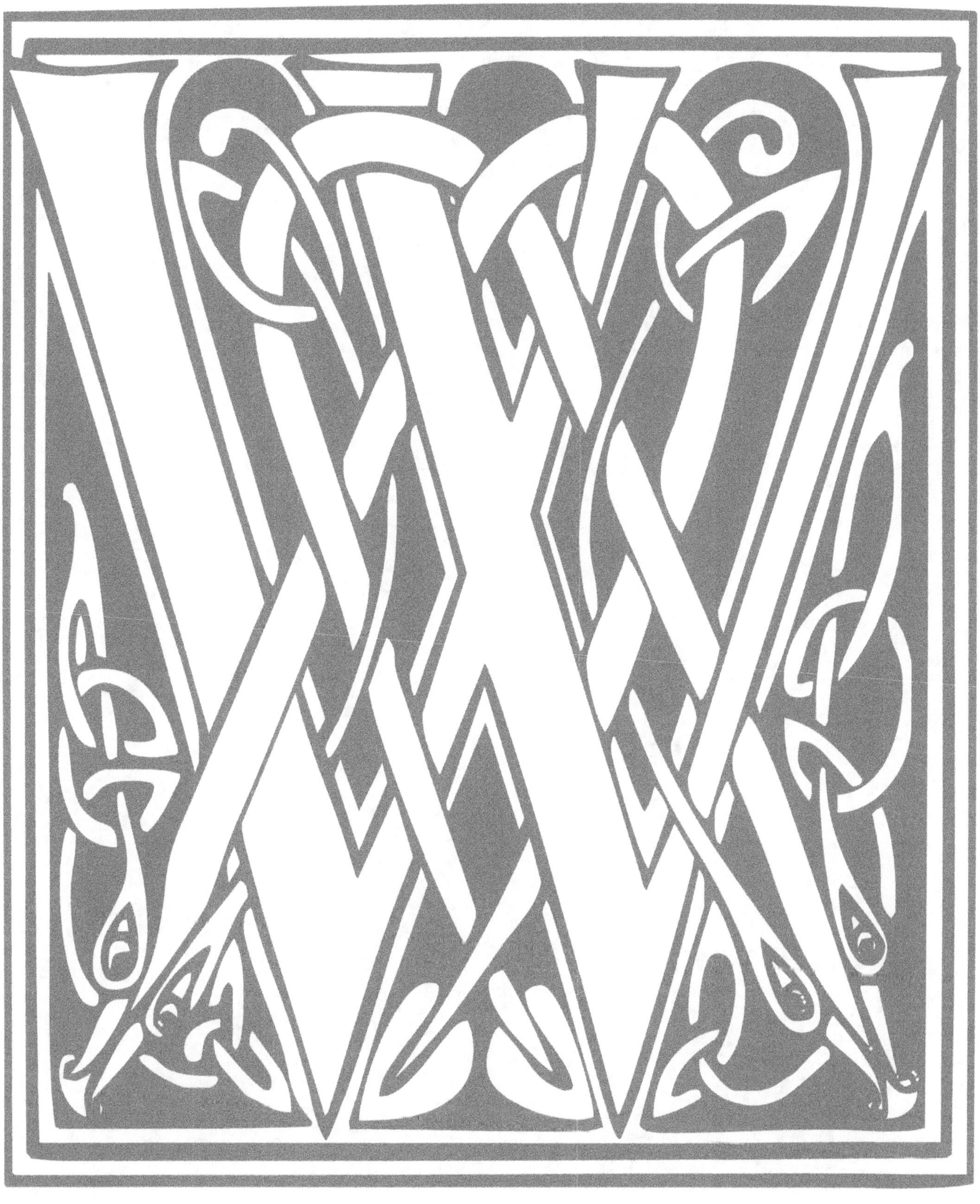

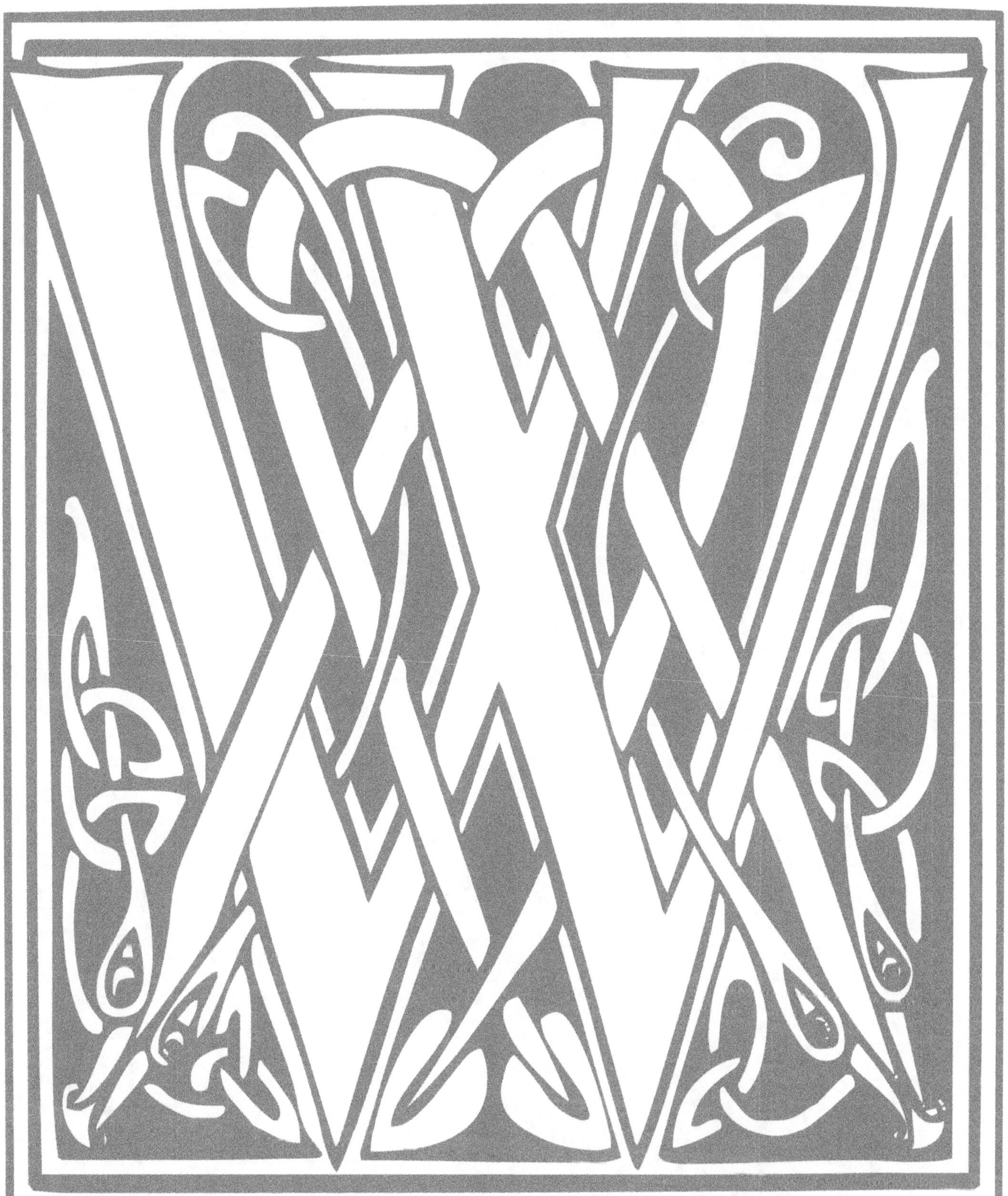

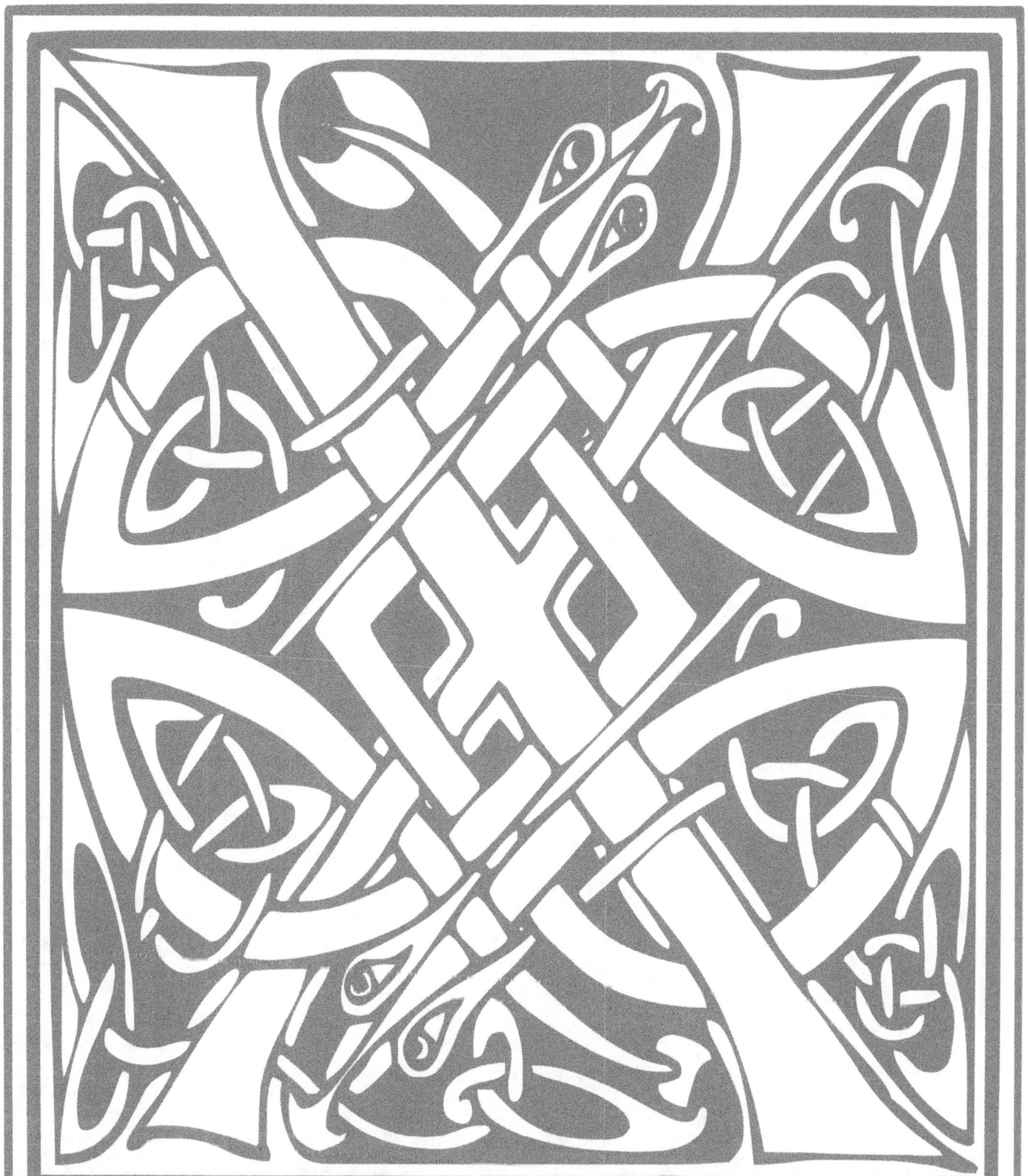

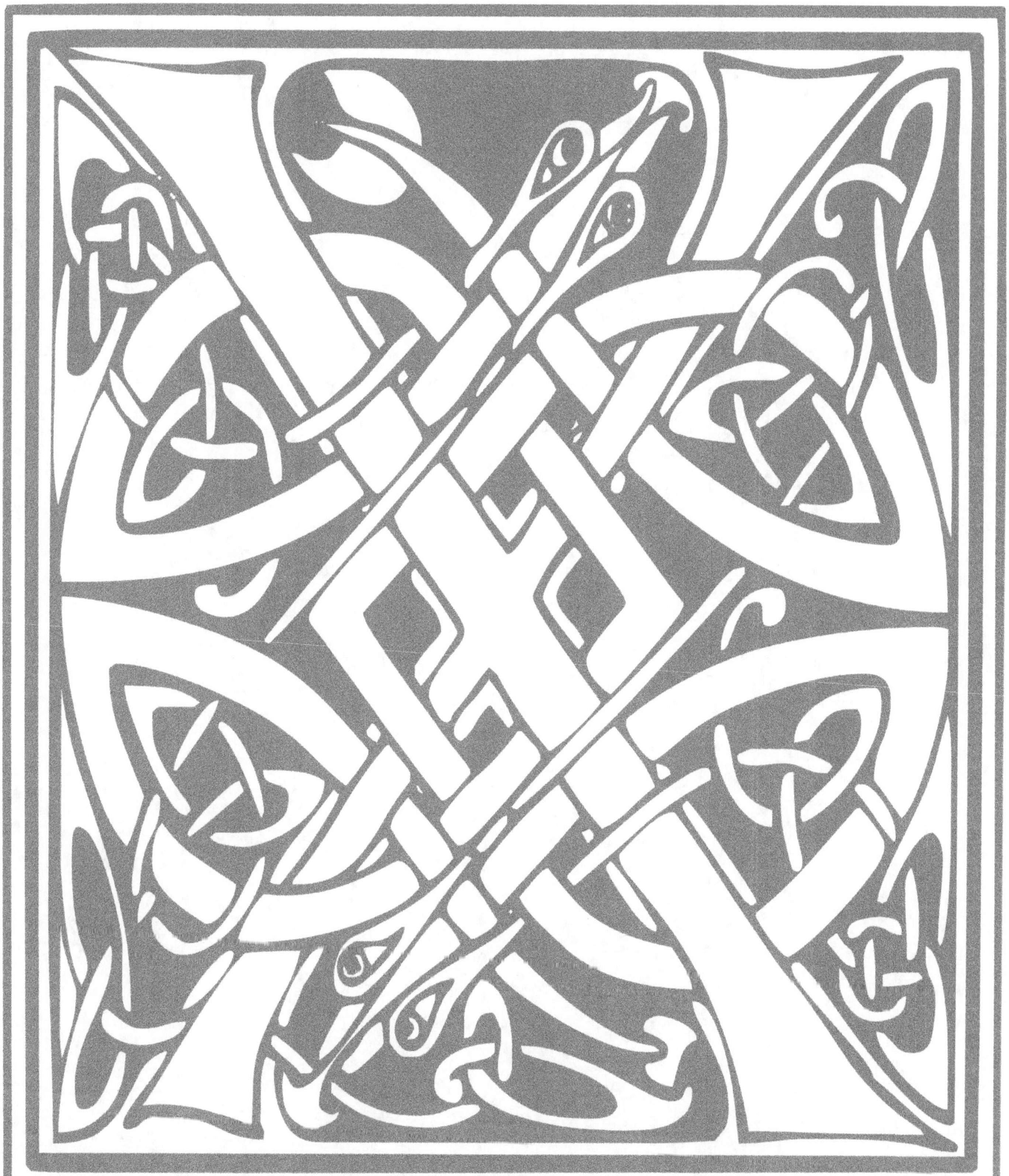

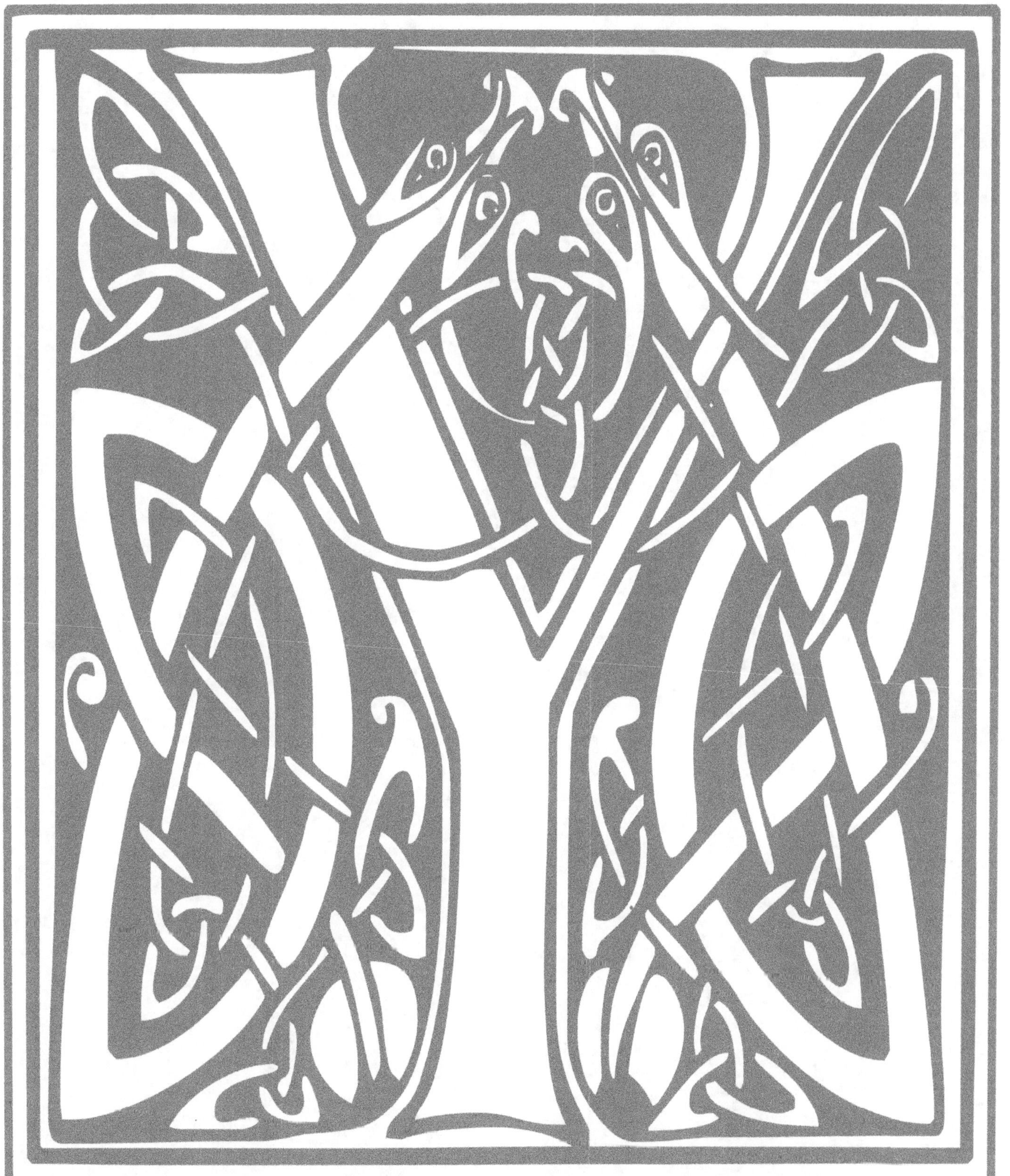

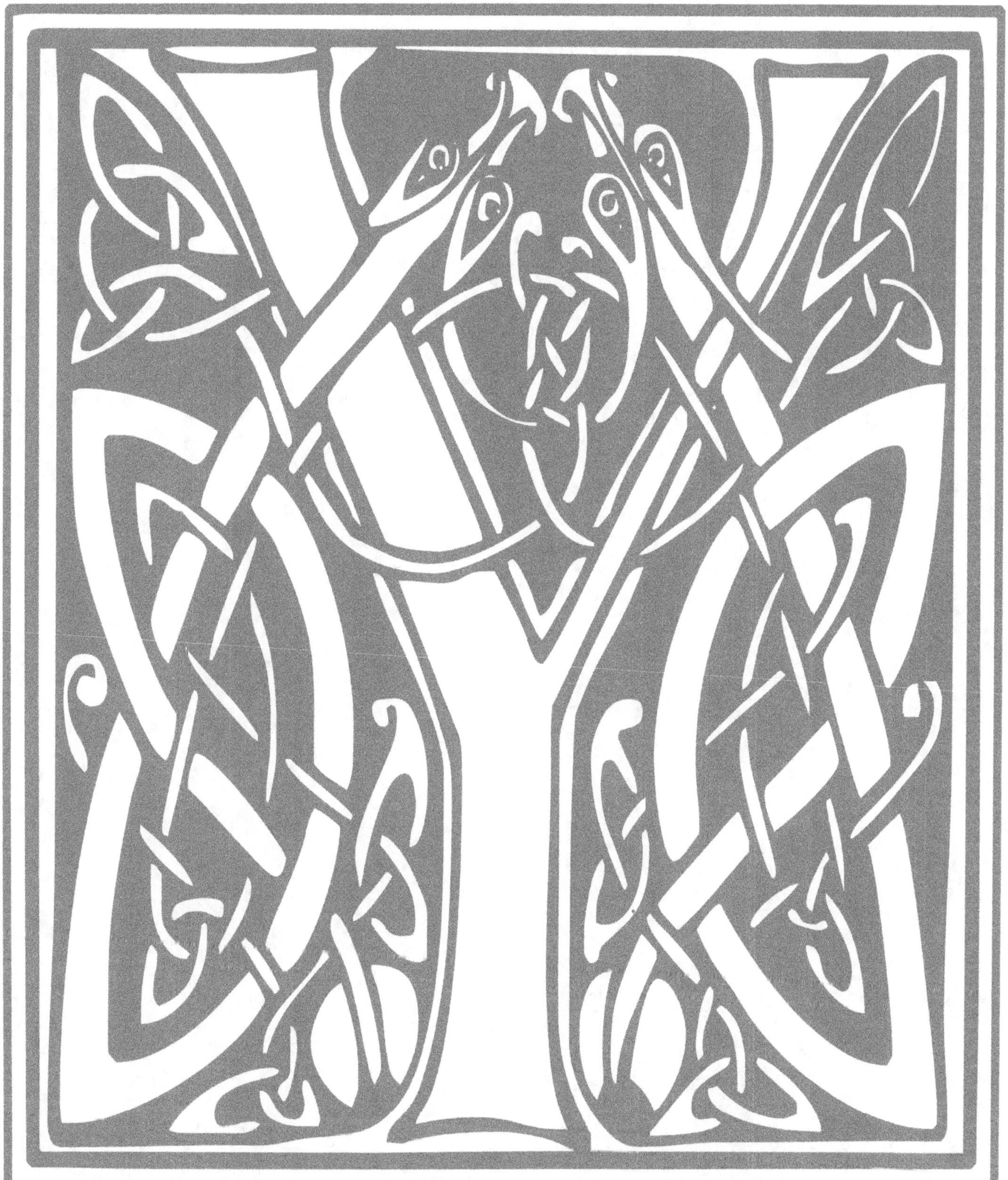

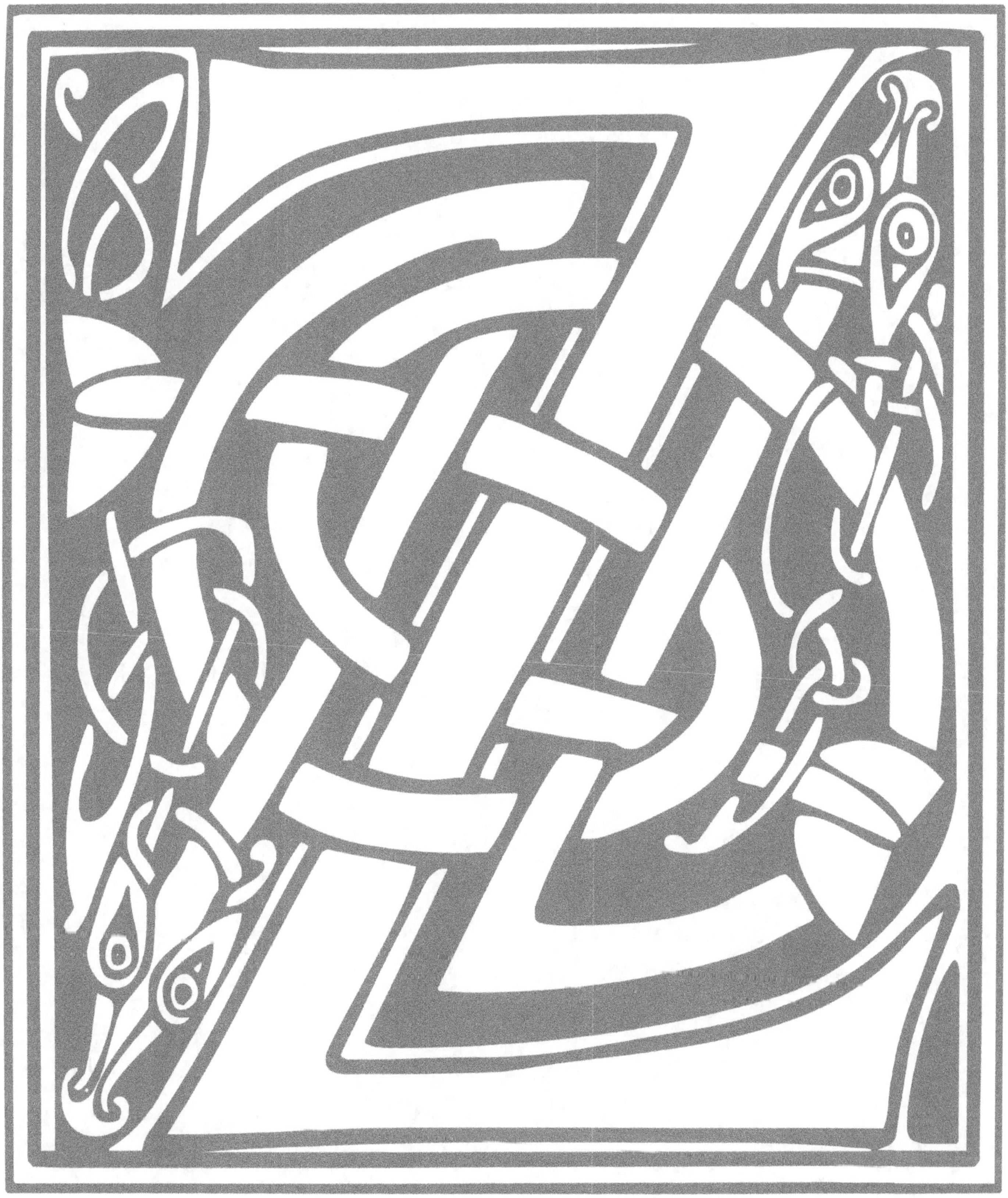

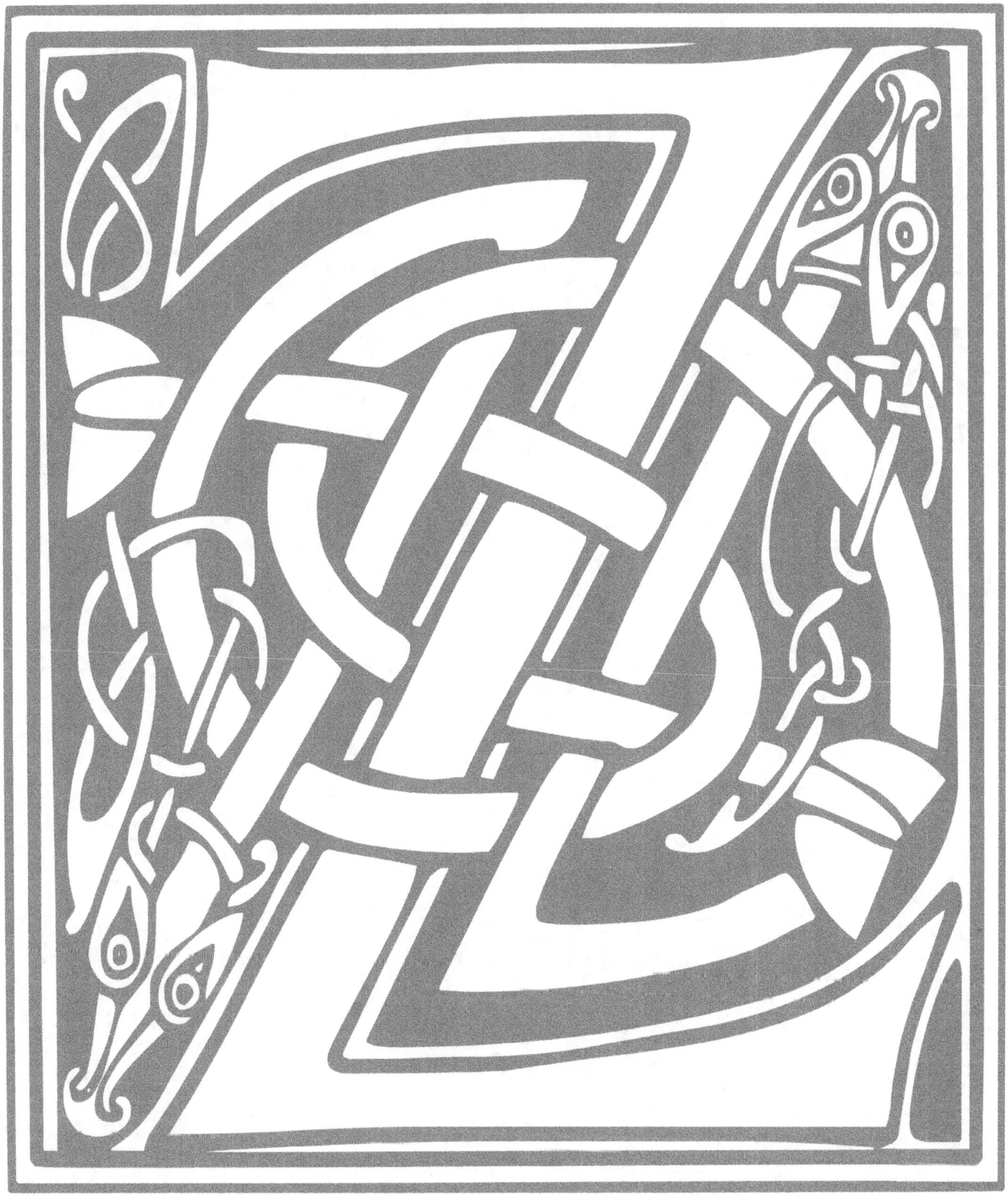

www.ingramcontent.com/pod-product-compliance
Lightning Source LLC
Chambersburg PA
CBHW080305180526
45167CB00006B/2682
* 9 7 8 1 5 4 4 0 8 3 5 5 1 *